Crime Prevention and Social Control

edited by
Ronald L. Akers
Edward Sagarin

Published in Cooperation with
the American Society of Criminology

The Praeger Special Studies program—utilizing the most modern and efficient book production techniques and a selective worldwide distribution network—makes available to the academic, government, and business communities significant, timely research in U.S. and international economic, social, and political development.

Crime Prevention and Social Control

PRAEGER SPECIAL STUDIES IN U.S. ECONOMIC, SOCIAL, AND POLITICAL ISSUES

Praeger Publishers   New York   Washington   London

Library of Congress Cataloging in Publication Data

Interamerican Congress of Criminology, 2d, Caracas,
    1972.
    Crime prevention and social control.

    (Praeger special studies in U.S. economic, social,
and political issues)
    "Published in cooperation with the American Society of
Criminology."
    Bibliography: p.
    1. Crime prevention—Congresses.   2. Police—
Congresses.   3. Criminal justice, Administration of—
Congresses.   I. Akers, Ronald L., ed.   II. Sagarin,
Edward, 1913-   ed.   III. American Society of Crimi-
nology.   IV. Title.
HV6010.I47 1972   364.4   74-5743
ISBN 0-275-28850-1

PRAEGER PUBLISHERS
111 Fourth Avenue, New York, N.Y. 10003, U.S.A.
5, Cromwell Place, London SW7 2JL, England

Published in the United States of America in 1974
by Praeger Publishers, Inc.

In November 1972, the Second Inter-American Congress of Criminology was held in Caracas, Venezuela. Sponsored by the American Society of Criminology, together with other international and Latin American organizations, it saw several hundred scholars, primarily concerned with crime, delinquency, deviant behavior, and corrections, gather together to present papers and exchange views.

The present volume is a selection of papers that were delivered at the Caracas meeting, whose Program Chairman was Edward Sagarin, a co-editor of the volume. It is one of a series of books coming out of that meeting, and is published in response to a demand that the research information, data, ideas, and proposals heard at Caracas be made permanently available to professionals, students, government officials and others engaged in the effort to understand the phenomenon of crime in modern society.

For the record, the officers of the American Society of Criminology at the time of the Caracas meeting were:

President: Dr. Charles L. Newman
President-Elect: Dr. John C. Ball
Vice-President: Dr. Edward Sagarin
Vice-President: Dr. Nicholas Kittrie
Secretary-Treasurer: Dr. Sawyer F. Sylvester

CONTENTS

INTRODUCTION

It is a broad umbrella indeed under which we have grouped the small number of brief papers in this volume: Crime Prevention and Social Control. The concept of social control refers to all those actions of socialization, formal and informal application of social sanctions and other practices in a society intended to encourage conformity and discourage deviance from prevailing social norms. The papers included here, obviously, touch only on formal control of crime and delinquency through the criminal justice system. Crime prevention, stopping crime before it occurs, is a narrower concept subsumed under social control, but is itself general enough to be open to several meanings. Both specific deterrence (deterring the one to whom sanctions have been applied from committing further criminal acts) and general deterrence (deterring others who are potential offenders from criminal behavior by the example of sanctioning apprehended violators) may be viewed as types of prevention, since both are intended to prevent future criminal activity. However, prevention has usually been given a somewhat different definition, namely actions taken to forestall crime beyond or instead of the threatening or the application of legal penalties. Thus, such procedures as the removal of environmental or personal causes of crime, technological "hardening" of the crime target, and reducing opportunities for crime, various kinds of police and citizen actions to thwart crime before it is completed, and intervention programs with populations specifically identified as having high potential for crime or delinquency—all are examples of this kind of prevention.

Given the complexity of the issues which would fall within these concepts of prevention and control, it would be pretentious to claim that the papers in this volume cover all aspects of crime prevention, apprehension of the transgressor, adjudication of guilt or innocence in the courts, and other questions, each with its own ramifications. However, in the contributions included here, important issues are raised, clarified, and studied. They add to our knowledge and, along with other scientific, scholarly, and applied literature in the field, deserve our apt attention if solutions to the knotty problems of crime facing modern societies are to be found.

We have divided the papers into three major areas of concern. In the first section, five criminologists approach the issues of crime prevention and deterrence from diverse vantage points. In the first selection, Jerome Himelhoch attempts to integrate the psychological and social factors in the development of youths who are of lower-class origin and find themselves impelled toward or on the verge of criminal careers. It is a complex and highly synthetic structure that Himelhoch offers, bringing together the work of numerous others in the field (not only those mentioned and to whom a debt is acknowledged, but others associated with learning, opportunity-temptation, and labeling theories). What is interesting here is that the author draws from his model of causation the implications for crime prevention or reduction; and while a theorist is not obligated to do this, one cannot but be indebted to him if he does.

The rest of the papers in this section deal with the theoretical and methodological issues involved in studying the deterrent effect of legal penalties on crime. Douglas Cousineau is mainly concerned with some methodological difficulties that have hampered previous students of deterrence, or have been ignored by them. What if there is a time lag between the moment that sanctions take effect and the moment that they have their impact on the crime-prone population? What methods must be utilized to have a homogeneous population base line, so that the effects of legal sanctions can be properly compared? Cousineau offers some suggestions for overcoming these and other difficulties. His search for homogeneity may assist researchers who in the future grapple with the question of the relationship of legal sanctions to crime reduction.

The paper by William Bowers raises questions that have a long history and yet have received little attention: for instance, even if punishment is not effective as a deterrent, does it serve other purposes? Among the other probable functions of punishment, he takes note of repression, retribution, and dominance over a minority group. Such purposes may be seen as socially useful by one sector of a society and as oppressive by others. The implications of this work are readily seen: that punishment is at best a mixed bag, and at worst an instrument of oppression that does not even succeed in its manifest and avowed aim. Bowers himself does not draw these conclusions; he suggests the bypaths and byproducts of punishment that must be investigated if logical and valid research is to be pursued.

Stanley Grupp examines deterrence in the specific area of marihuana smoking. Marihuana smoking is an example of a larger group of offenses called "crimes without victims" and crimes which are mala prohibita—wrong only because they are prohibited, rather than because they present any inherent injury to others or to society. Thus, a significant number of people have not internalized strong moral injunctions against marihuana use. On the other hand, few engage in it because of strong ideological reason, as in the case of certain political crime. The question, then, becomes: Does legal prohibition and the possibility of criminal sanctions deter use of marihuana? Grupp approaches the question with demographic cohorts, sophisticated study of significant variables, and knowledge of the area. His conclusions throw light on more than deterrence of marihuana smoking, although application of his findings must be made with great caution to areas of behavior amenable to greater social pressure, less peer group support, more moral dilemma, greater ideological commitment, and other factors that enter into this complex picture.

Finally, in this section on deterrence, we offer the essay by Richard Henshel. His thesis is simple, but constitutes a telling challenge to much previous work on the efficacy of punishment as a deterrent (particularly the work on capital punishment). In brief, he demands that the factor of the extent to which the tempted or incipient offender had knowledge of the nature, celerity, certainty, and severity of the punishment be taken into account in studying this problem. His essay, like Merton's famous work on the self-fulfilling prophesy, might well have started with the oft-quoted dictum of W. I. Thomas, "If men define situations as real, they are real in their consequences." In this case, Henshel would contend that it is the extent to which a situation is defined as real by certain men that the consequences of that situation will be felt.

The six articles in the second section relate to the police. They range in scope, some highlighting police efficiency, others examining police corruption. We start with a study of the characteristics of police and how these characteristics are related to later job performance. In this paper, Bernard Cohen reports on age, education, IQ, grades on civil service examinations, and many other factors. It is difficult to see how a work of this sort can be overlooked in the United States, at a time when the upgrading of police is a primary consideration in the struggle against crime.

In a study conducted in Canada, Clifford Shearing reports on the telephone calls made to the police for assistance, the response, the nature of the reported difficulty, and some conclusions drawn by both the police and the researcher on such calls. At a time when "dial-a-cop" has become more frequent in many American cities, studies of this sort must be followed with great care. Are there false alarms, as in the case of fire, and are there possibilities that this will become a form of harassment or, worse, a means of deflecting police from one criminal scene by sending them elsewhere? Can every call be answered by sending a patrol car, and if not, what criteria for making judgments should be used?

Two papers deal with relationships between the police and minority groups, a matter of significance in many countries of the world, but particularly so in the United States. For Roger Baldwin, it is a matter of reciprocal suspicion, and one might add that such a situation seldom (perhaps never) remains static. It improves or deteriorates, as the case may be, and for improvement, or de-escalation of the suspicion, it may require social planning, education, and deliberate moves from both sides. The manner in which this suspicion exists in one community, the Puerto Rican area of New York, is described by Wayne Cotton. Here, Cotton finds a new and young leadership arising; it challenges not the police as such, but the utilization of police forces in a manner that does not grasp the complexities of the Hispanic culture. Both of these papers compel one to examine the oft-made proposals of community control of police and of the desirability (or undesirability) of the assignment of police that reflect the ethnic backgrounds of the residents of a ghetto or even of a malintegrated area.

In general, Emilio Viano sees a need for change in the discretionary police practices regarding victimless crime, particularly prostitution and homosexuality. Present methods make for the possibility of blackmail or extortion (whether by plainclothesmen or those masquerading as such), a poor deployment of police forces, and great psychological damage without concomitant reduction in the putative social evils that they are designed to control.

Then there is the matter of police corruption. The fact of corruption no one would deny; it is the extent of it that is often debated. Julian Roebuck and Thomas Barker do not address that issue. Instead, they analyze types of police corruption, putting forth what we believe is the first such typology. It is ambitious and all-encompassing, and it may be possible to use such a typology as a starting point to determine the measures available to diminish each type of corruption.

We conclude the volume with three papers in an area the importance of which cannot be overestimated: namely, the administration of criminal justice and the functioning of the courts. Criminal court delay is notorious in the United States. It is sometimes requested by defendants, sometimes by prosecution, and in the case of the poor, the accused are often in local lockups awaiting trial, with pernicious effects on others, particularly if they have families. Edward Green examines this question in a study conducted in a small industrial city; whether his findings would be applicable to New York, Chicago, or Philadelphia, it is difficult to know, but the study is worth replication in a larger area. He uses as variables race and type of occupation, and relates them to crimes against the person, those against property, and all other crimes.

It is generally agreed that a veritable revolution in juvenile court procedure was initiated by the Supreme Court decision in the Gault case, but it appears thus far that it has been an aborted revolution at best, and perhaps a counterrevolution, at worst. If ever there were an area of the handling of offenders that cries out for rehabilitation, it is with the young. Yet, so little is accomplished, although the society spends considerable sums and goes through quite some motions. Sue Titus Reid examines this question, and comes up largely with the hope that both the granting of due process to juveniles in the court system and the use of the approach of individualized treatment (the original "big brother" philosophy which has been so severely criticized by Anthony Platt) could prove effective. Her argument is cogent, although many look with suspicion on the individualized treatment approach which means, in effect, that youths of higher social class families, and those who are white and well educated, are almost invariably better treated than those born to less fortunate circumstances.

Finally, Peter Lejins presents two models of prevention and control in the criminal justice system. One he calls the "systemic planning and evaluation model," and it would take into account several features of crime control: the removal of the causes of crime (quite a big order), the mechanical protection of society (largely the question of police, although there can be environmental design for protection as well), and punitive sanctions (back to deterrence). To this, he proposes what her terms a "composite planning model," which involves the broader cultural context in which crime and crime control exist, and social action programs, their costs and standards. It is in the elaboration of these two models, their implications and implementation, that Lejins sees a step forward in the reduction of crime and the handling of the offender.

The articles, of course, speak for themselves; we have merely sought to highlight some of their main features. Their ultimate significance will be evaluated by those who read them and by future research. They move us toward an understanding of prevention, deterrence, and control of crime and delinquency. If they also inspire others to continue efforts to reach that understanding, then they will have accomplished their mission and we will have achieved our objective in assembling them.

R.L.A. and E.S.

PART

I

CRIME PREVENTION
AND DETERRENCE

1

A PSYCHOSOCIAL MODEL
FOR THE REDUCTION OF
LOWER-CLASS YOUTH CRIME
Jerome Himelhoch

In this paper I shall present an integrative psychosocial model of crime causation and then suggest some of its implications for the reduction of predatory offenses by youthful lower-class males, particularly those in black and Latin American ghettos. Although I am indebted to Reckless (1961), Knudten (1970), Cohen (1966), and Cohen and Short (1971), I have attempted a new inclusive synthesis which integrates learning, psychodynamic, symbolic interactionist, control, subcultural, opportunity structure, social disorganization, and labeling perspectives. Hopefully, my model will sensitize social scientists and practitioners to a set of interrelated variables which must be taken into account in understanding crime causation and control. Technically, my model is not a theory because I do not specify the causal order of the variables, although I do occasionally suggest the causal priority of certain variables.

A Psychosocial Model of Crime and
Delinquency Causation

According to my model everyman or everywoman acts in a psychosocial field which may be represented by the concentric zones and sectors diagrammed in Figure 1.1. His personality is divided into Zone 1, an inner core containing his motives, capacities, and self-

This research was financed in part by grants from the Ford Foundation, the University of Missouri-St. Louis Office of Research, and Public Health Service grants MHO7287 - 01, -01S1, -02A1. I wish to thank Sherif el Hakim for his comments on an earlier draft.

FIGURE 1.1 Diagram of Psychosocial Field

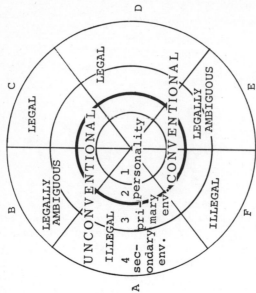

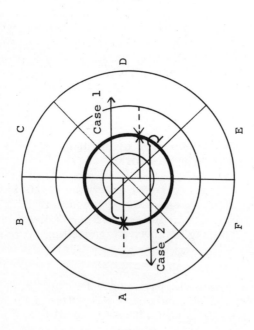

Case 1. Would be offender, reformed by conventional primary controls and legitimate opportunity. Becomes conformist.

Case 2. "Innovator" blocked by absence of legitimate opportunity. Labeled. Becomes career offender.

4

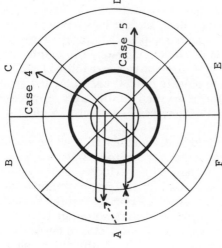

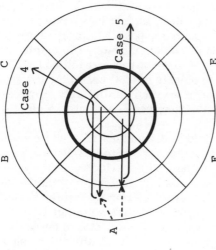

Case 3. Unconventional person, legally ambiguous action. Labeled Becomes career offender.

Case 4. Offender reformed by criminal justice system. Adopts unconventional but legal career.

Case 5. Would be offender. Deterred by criminal justice system. Becomes conformist.

5

concept, and the surrounding Zone 2 which provides him with inner controls. Zone 3 is his primary environment of face-to-face informal relationships, while Zone 4 is his secondary environment of formal interaction in bureaucratic organizations.

The primary and secondary groups and institutions provide the individual with reference objects (reference groups and role models), informal and formal social controls, and legitimate or illegitimate opportunity structures. The basic postulate of my paradigm is that the individual's behavior can be explained by the criminogenic-anticriminogenic balance of his motives, capacities, self-concept, inner controls, reference objects, social controls, and opportunity structures. The behavior of a group of similarly situated persons can be explained by those of the above elements which they have in common.

The psychosocial field is divided not only into concentric zones, but also into six sectors, which vary in terms of legality and conventionality, as defined by general American conduct norms. The sectors vary in form and content by society, subculture, and time period. Action proceeding leftward from the center to the periphery in Sector A is illegal and unconventional; while an act moving to the right in D is legal and conventional. In Sector B action is unconventional and legally ambiguous; in C unconventional but legal. Action in E is conventional, but legally ambiguous; while action in F is conventional but illegal. Acts in E and F are committed by respectable and relatively powerful persons such as police officers, presidents, and corporation executives.

The assumption underlying my model, as diagrammed in Figure 1.1, is that the individual may begin an action sequence or career in one sector, but upon perceiving obstacles in that sector and/or greater attractions in another sector, may reverse himself and move into the second sector. The obstacles are strong internal or social controls or lack of opportunity or absence of reinforcement by reference objects. The attractions are weaker controls or greater opportunities and more reinforcement by reference objects in the other sector. This combination of push from one sector and pull into another is represented by the dotted line. The solid line shows the individual's original outward progress into a sector, his encounter with an opposing force, his reversal as the action reenters the intrapsychic zones (1 and 2) where he reevaluates the situation and his self-concept, and his subsequent new action sequence or career in a different sector.

To illustrate some of the possibilities, I have diagrammed five hypothetical cases, one of which I shall explain for purposes of illustration. In case 4 one might have a transgressor reformed by a wise probation officer who helps his client find a legitimate job, but tolerates his unconventional lifestyle, dress, and friends.

Such progressions within a single sector or movement into a different sector can refer either to an individual's short-run action sequence or to his career. They can also refer to culturally patterned careers determined by the common modal personality and the shared primary and secondary environments of a group of similarly situated individuals. To plan a program for the reduction of youth crime, one must discover the particular combination of social and psychological variables which cause a given category of youngsters to persist in a law-abiding career or to move from a delinquent to a law-abiding career.

It appears likely that the highest rates of serious predatory delinquency and youth crime are found in large homogeneous black and Latin American ghettos, although rates are also high in certain lower-class white slums (Boggs, 1970). For adolescent males there is some theoretical and empirical basis for several hypotheses which explain how the primary and secondary environments in the ghetto produce a strongly criminogenic balance of the variables in my model. Demoralized multi-problem families rear children with weak inner controls, whom the parents cannot effectively restrain (weak primary social controls). Moreover, police brutality and corruption and low community cohesion engender weak secondary social controls. School failure, rejection by middle-class teachers, unemployment and underemployment and other class and racist denials of legitimate opportunities produce unfavorable self-concepts and aggressive motives. Absence of successful father figures causes sex-role anxiety and compensatory machismo; while the outmigration of middle-class blacks deprives the boys of conventional role models and reference objects. Finally, organized crime and delinquent subcultures provide illegitimate opportunity structures and criminal reference objects.

Implications of the Model for the Reduction of Lower-Class Youth Crime

Preventive measures may simultaneously be classified according to three considerations: targets and methods, superficiality, and conservatism.

In regard to targets and methods, the following strategies can be distinguished: individual treatment of offenders or "potential offenders" by casework, counseling, or psychotherapy; group work or community organization with neighborhood primary and secondary groups and institutions, such as the family, the school, the gang, law enforcement and criminal justice, social agencies, etc. or with the neighborhood as a whole through area projects; and political action at the national, state or local governmental level to produce changes in the primary and secondary organization of the neighborhoods.

According to the second system of classification, preventive measures may involve short-run, remedial, and symptomatic treatment or long-run, basic institutional modification to alter primary and secondary environments. The latter approach attempts to remove the supposed "underlying causes" of lower-class delinquency and youth crime.

Finally, the basic goal of preventive measures may be to protect the status quo or to transform existing patterns of racial and class stratification. One reason for the failure of many programs has been an ambiguity about "Whose side are you on?" Too often practitioners find themselves on the side of law and order in the service of the power structure. Moreover, they often concern themselves with the adolescent status offenses and victimless crimes, instead of concentration upon serious predatory offenses. Such goals as support of the power structure and of puritanical morality are likely to turn off lower-class minority youth.

In either prevention or rehabilitation, we should discover the criminogenic variables which can be manipulated with the least expenditure of effort and the least resistance from powerful vested interests and which have the greatest multiplier effect on other variables. For example, it may be easier to change formal rather than informal social controls. Moreover, it may be more feasible to shift the balance between legitimate and illegitimate opportunities than to recast reference objects. Perhaps it is easier to influence the peer group through guided group interaction or a detached worker program than to reorder the interpersonal relations in the family. These psychosocial system modifications are important in regard to the reduction of serious career delinquency and youth crime. Several writers have stressed the casual, episodic, and adventitious character of many delinquent acts (Briar and Piliavin, 1965; Short and Strodtbeck, 1965). In such circumstances a relatively superficial change in the contingencies of the action situation may be sufficient. Examples would be technological measures to "harden the target" or to increase the visibility of burglary or automobile theft.

One condition for effective primary and secondary social controls is that they reinforce conventional inner controls. This is more likely to occur when the individual feels positive affect toward the agents and recognizes an identity of interest with them. His inner controls will also be strengthened if he is given responsibility to make decisions on his own. Moreover, the greater his investment in a favorable self-concept, a successful role or career, acceptance by a conventional reference group, and material possessions, and, up to a point, the more he has been rewarded, the less likely is he to jeopardize these investments by flouting the control agents. Effective social control requires that agents, such as teachers, parents, peers, and police, present a consistent moral front. Finally, a cohesive local community, integrated around generally pro-legal values, will reduce the rate of youth crime.

Crucial to the strength and direction of inner controls is the degree of commitment to conventional or unconventional roles, groups, and norms. Independent researches on high school students by Hirschi (1969) and myself (Himelhoch, 1968) indicate that strength of attachment to future conventional roles and groups, such as college for a high school student, typically serves as an inhibitor of delinquency. One influence upon the strength of inner controls is the presence or absence of learned rationalizations which neutralize taboos against infraction.

I shall now turn to a few specific proposals:

1. The highest priority should be placed upon political action to move municipal, state, and particularly the federal government to undertake massive reforms in income distribution, employment, taxation, housing, criminal justice, health, education, and welfare. One prerequisite for such action is probably the politico-economic organization of the poor. To reduce lower-class youthful street crime, the ghetto must be transformed so that it ceases to be a large, stigmatized, involuntarily segregated, homogeneous population living in substandard conditions.

Ghetto famllies, including the poorest ones, must be enabled to move wherever they wish, including integrated middle-class suburbs. Job training and placement, particularly for unemployed out-of-school minority youths, preferential hiring to offset previous discrimination, family income maintenance plans in lieu of welfare, rent subsidies, housing loans, and scattersite small housing projects are necessary measures.

Fleisher (1966) has presented convincing evidence that a moderate increase in employment or income would markedly reduce delinquency among white and nonwhite lower-class youth. In support of the proposal for the facilitation of emigration from slum areas, it can be pointed out that several researches suggest that the dispersion of slum residents reduces their delinquency rate (Clark and Wenninger, 1962; Reiss and Rhodes, 1961).

Concurrent with the facilitation of lower-class emigration, black and white middle- and upper-class persons, including college students and faculty, should be encouraged by economic and cultural incentives to work and live in the inner city. Significant economic development could bring in commercial, small manufacturing, educational, governmental, and entertainment enterprises. These should not be small upper-status enclaves, but should be evenly dispersed throughout the depressed area. Extra policing, civilian patrols, good lighting and other short-run crime prevention measures would probably be

necessary to reassure the new migrants. Once a large number of
persons had reason to use the streets, there might be informal social
controls, which Jane Jacobs (1961) calls "eyes on the streets" to discourage crime.

2. In order to reduce serious predatory offenses, it is important
to decriminalize most of the "crime without victims" (drug use,
drunkenness, abortion, homosexuality, gambling, and prostitution),
public order offenses (vagrancy and disorderly conduct), and the adolescent status offenses (truancy, curfew violation, incorrigibility,
running away, "growing up in idleness and crime," and precocious
drinking, cursing, and copulation). In terms of the diagram in Figure
1.1, the unconventional-legal sector would be enlarged at the expense
of the unconventional-legally ambiguous and the unconventional-illegal
sectors.

With regard to victimless crimes, there are many advantages
in decriminalization. The illegitimate opportunity structure of organized crime would be enormously weakened. Police corruption would
be reduced and the overloaded criminal justice system freed to concentrate upon predatory offenses. Addicts would avoid criminal labelling and would be freed from the pressure to push dope, rob, pimp,
or steal to support their habit. They would not need to turn to drug
subcultures for a steady source of supply.

The repeal of the statutes proscribing adolescent status offenses,
along with the provision of meaningful adult roles, would lessen adolescent status discontent as a possible cause of delinquency. Moreover,
delinquent labelling would also be avoided. With regard to both the
adolescent status offenses and the victimless crimes, where the behavior in question does have some social or psychological costs, the
person should receive help, without judicial coercion, by friends,
family, voluntary associations, or formal health, educational, or
welfare organizations.

3. The slum school, with its inadequate facilities, overworked,
often poorly prepared teachers and preoccupation with discipline,
frequently resembles a minimum security correctional institution.
Coming from family backgrounds deficient in middle-class verbal
skills, the children often feel frustrated, angry, humiliated, and alien-
ated. School failure is closely related to self-derogation and delinquency. To remedy these defects, a number of the recommendations
of the President's Commission on Law Enforcement and the Administration of Justice (1967) make sense: greater financial support,
less punitive means of dealing with behavior problems, instructional
material relevant to inner city life, encouraging college aspirations
for qualified students, realistic vocational training, placement, and
work-release programs for those not going to college, involvement
of the local community in teaching and administration, and reduction

of racial and economic segregation. Local community control and bussing to achieve desegregation may, however, prove to be incompatible goals.

Any measures to lessen the likelihood of school failure will presumably reduce delinquency. Some thought should be given to the abolition or moderation of the competitive grading system, which necessitates the failure of some students. Moreover, special resources and efforts should be devoted to assist the unsuccessful student. Perhaps teachers should be specially rewarded for their ability to help the least able students improve their performance.

It is possible for skillful teachers to get lower-class adolescents actively engaged in the discovery of knowledge and in creative self-expression. School can be a meaningful experience, rather than compulsory passive participation in an authoritarian ritual. In this social climate, the student can identify with the teacher as a law-abiding but not necessarily square adult role model. To the extent to which it is possible to create these conditions, the student is more likely to acquire needed skills for legitimate roles, learn responsibility and autonomy, and develop a favorable self-concept and more adequate inner control.

4. Concurrent with political action for basic institutional reform, it is desirable on the local community level to have demonstration projects, with rigorous evaluative research, to test the impact of preventive programs utilizing recreation, detached workers, area projects, the mass media, and religious activities. It will help the objective of politico-economic organization of the poor if demonstration projects and social services are administered by indigenous reform-oriented organizations (as welfare rights organizations, tenants' leagues, consumer protection groups, counseling and referral services run by local residents, and consumer cooperatives).

Thorough reform of the entire criminal justice system is necessary in order to gain the confidence of ghetto residents, deter crime, and apprehend offenders. In particular the police need adequate training in interpersonal relations, should be subject to a considerable measure of local community control, and should be integrated into the informal social system of the neighborhood. It may facilitate the community integration of the police if the latter work with civilian youth patrols. I have heard reports, unsupported by research, that such patrols, recruited from notorious delinquents, have successfully reduced street crime in several St. Louis neighborhoods.

While the family is of crucial importance as a socializing agency and a primary social control, Rodman and Grams (1967) contend that the slum family can best be strengthened by improved income, occupational opportunity, education, and housing, to which one might add the urgent need to give lower-class women the same access to contraception that middle- and upper-class women now have. A reduction in

11

fertility might have far-reaching indirect effects in strengthening the family, increasing living standards, improving child-rearing, lessening frustration and aggression, reducing school classes, diminishing gangs, bringing about more favorable self-concepts and stronger inner and outer controls, with relatively greater influence of parents as against peers.

5. Stringent gun control legislation is necessary to reduce the peculiarly American universal opportunity structure for homicide, assault, robbery, and other crimes of violence. It may, however, take thousands of homicides and several more assassinations before the gun lobby can be defeated.

6. Except in unusual cases, I doubt the efficacy of individual casework or psychotherapy for the prevention of delinquency. The "early identification" approach which labels and often segregates alleged "predelinquents" for treatment of untested effectiveness is more likely to cause than to prevent crime. There is, moreover, the danger of putting the youngster in the sick role, thereby freeing him from responsibility for his actions. To reorder a child's motives, self-concept, and inner controls requires that one replace or reeducate his reference objects, open new legitimate opportunities while blocking illegitimate ones, and counteract the stigmatizing, ego-damaging responses of punitive primary and secondary social controls.

Conclusions

The integrative model of crime and delinquency causation depicts the individual as acting in a psychosocial field defined by concentric circles representing personality, primary environment, and secondary environment. The field is also defined by six sectors which vary according to conventionality and legality. The individual's behavior can be explained by the criminogenic-anticriminogenic balance of his motives, capacities, self-concept, inner controls, reference objects, social controls, and opportunity structures.

The characteristics of the black or Latin American ghetto create a criminogenic combination of the above elements, resulting in high rates of predatory offenses by young males. Several proposals for the reduction of such offenses, so that the young men would be helped to avoid or to move from the illegal-unconventional sector and to remain in or move into the legally ambiguous-unconventional sector, the legal-unconventional sector or the legal-conventional sector, can be derived from the model. Personality modification requires changes in the primary environment, which in turn necessitates reconstruction of the secondary environment. This leads to several proposals, including the transformation of the ghetto, decriminalization of victimless crimes and adolescent status offenses, and educational reform.

References

Boggs, Sarah L.
  1970   Urban crime patterns. In Daniel Glaser (ed.), Crime in the
          City. New York: Harper and Row.

Briar, Scott, and Irving Piliavin
  1965   Delinquency, situational inducements, and commitment to
          conformity. Social Problems, 13: 35-45.

Clark, John P., and Eugene P. Wenninger
  1962   Socio-economic class and area as correlates of illegal be-
          havior among juveniles. American Sociological Review, 27:
          826-34.

Cohen, Albert K.
  1966   Deviance and Control. Englewood Cliffs, N.J.: Prentice-
          Hall.

Cohen, Albert K., and James F. Short, Jr.
  1971   Crime and juvenile delinquency. In Robert K. Merton and
          Robert Nisbet (eds.), Contemporary Social Problems. New
          York: Harcourt, Brace, Jovanovich.

Fleisher, Belton
  1966   The Economics of Delinquency. Chicago: Quadrangle.

Himelhoch, Jerome
  1968   Ambition, optimism and achievement among rural high
          school students. Mimeographed. University of Missouri-
          St. Louis.

Hirschi, Travis
  1969   Causes of Delinquency. Berkeley: University of California
          Press.

Jacobs, Jane
  1961   The Death and Life of Great American Cities. New York:
          Random House.

Knudten, Richard D.
  1970   Crime in a Complex Society. Homewood, Ill.: Dorsey Press.

President's Commission on Law Enforcement and Administration of Justice
  1967   The Challenge of Crime in a Free Society. Washington: Government Printing Office.

Reckless, Walter C.
  1961   A new theory of delinquency and crime. Federal Probation, 25(December): 42-46.

Reiss, Albert J., and Albert L. Rhodes
  1961   The distribution of juvenile delinquency in the social class structure. American Sociological Review, 26: 720-32.

Rodman, Hyman, and Paul Grams
  1967   Juvenile delinquency and the family: A review and discussion. In President's Commission on Law Enforcement and Administration of Justice. Task Force Report: Juvenile Delinquency and Youth Crime. Washington: Government Printing Office.

Short, James F., Jr., and Fred L. Strodtbeck
  1965   Group Process and Gang Delinquency. Chicago: University of Chicago Press.

2

A CRITIQUE OF THE
ECOLOGICAL APPROACH TO
THE STUDY OF DETERRENCE
Douglas F. Cousineau

Since 1968, there have been several significant attempts to study deterrence using the ecological approach (Gibbs, 1968; Tittle, 1969; Gray and Martin, 1969; Chiricos and Waldo, 1970; and Bailey, Gray and Martin, 1970). These studies have gone beyond the theoretical debates regarding the deterrent efficacy of sanctions, and have tried to examine directly the relationship between legal sanctions and crime rates. Indexes of the certainty and serverity of legal action are considered in terms of known offense rates for specific crimes, controlling for such basic ecological variables as age, sex, education, and level of urbanization. Other studies have also introduced controls for regional variations and racial compositions (Bean and Cushing, 1971) and have applied the same procedures to the analysis of Canadian data (Teevan, 1972). The social science approach to deterrence has been characterized by a great many assertions and abstract debates, and the pioneer researchers are to be commended for their efforts to examine the concept of deterrence with reference to empirical data. However, the nature of their data and the manner of their approach to it are such that the research is far from definitive and the conclusions offered must at best be considered moot. The purpose of the present paper is to examine several major limitations of the ecological approach as it has recently been applied to the study of deterrence, and to recommend some alternative research strategies which might facilitate the generation of more accurate and relevant data. Four major problems will be considered: first, the failure to differentiate between general and specific deterrence; second, the failure to take

This paper appeared in Social Science Quarterly 54 (June 1973), pp. 152-58, and is reprinted with permission.

into account problems of time lag; third, the failure to select appropriate base populations; and fourth, the failure to utilize homogeneous units of analysis.

Specific Versus General Deterrence

Throughout the theoretical literature, there is an underlying distinction between at least two kinds of deterrence: specific deterrence, which refers to the degree to which sanctions are effective in changing the behavior of a particular offender who is subjected to them; and general deterrence, which refers to the degree to which the sanctioning of offenders affects the behavior of potential offenders and/or the general public (Andenaes, 1966; Hawkins, 1971). Researchers using the ecological approach have failed to define deterrence, much less to differentiate between general and specific. Consequently, the indices which they employ are not sensitive to the distinction. The crime rates which are considered are typically based on the criminal convictions of all known offenders, regardless of their previous offense records. The rates of crime among first offenders in a population are valid indicators of general deterrence in that population, whereas the rates of crime among recidivists are indicators of the effectiveness or lack of it of specific deterrence. When the categories are combined, it is no longer justifiable to use the resulting crime rate as a measure of general deterrence. The problems of recidivism have already been explored in some depth (Wilkins, 1969) and there is no evidence that an ecological approach to this aspect of the problem would be especially useful. However, if crime rates were appropriately calculated on the basis of first offenders only, problems of general deterrence could be fruitfully explored, using this approach.

The Problem of Time Lag

Although theoretical discussions of general deterrence recognize that the effects of the punishment of offenders will require some period of time to become manifest in the behavior of the general public, most researchers using the ecological approach have failed to allow for an appropriate time lag between sanction and effect. For example, Tittle (1969) considers indices of crime and sanctions at only one point in time. Chiricos and Waldo (1970) do look for deterrent effects at several points in time, but they continue to compare indices for sanctions administered in one year with crime rates for the same year. They overlook the possibility that an increased severity of sanctions during 1950 may not have an impact on crime rates during 1950, but

16

may have a measurable impact in 1951 or 1952. Until the time lag
factor is taken into account, it is impossible to say whether or not a
deterrent effect has occurred. At least one researcher has made
systematic effort to consider the problem of time lag, although on a
very small scale. Schwartz (1968) considered rates of one crime,
that of rape, in one city at three separate points in time following an
increase in the severity of sanctions imposed. Future ecological
studies might usefully employ a similar methodology, hopefully taking
into account a wider variety of crimes over a much longer period of
time.

Selection of Base Line Populations

Some studies of deterrence make reference to crime rates which
are computed in terms of the incidence of crime in the general populations, an inappropriate base line for the consideration of crime statistics (Tittle, 1969). Many members of society are not eligible to commit certain crimes, and their rates of being charged with them or convicted of them will therefore be zero, regardless of how lenient or
how severe the legal sanctions are. As a minimum criterion, it is
important to consider the deterrent effects of sanctions of adult crimes
only in terms of crime rates for the population over the age of 18.
For some crime, only one sex is eligible to be considered criminal.
Thus, in evaluating the deterrent effects of legal sanctions for the
crime of rape, the appropriate base line for crime rates must be
restricted to the adult male population. Zimring and Hawkins (1968)
provide a useful extension of this approach when they suggest that for
every crime it is necessary to try to identify the criminal group and
the marginal group. In their usage, the criminal group refers to those
persons known to engage in the crime in question; the marginal group
refers to those persons who are like the criminal group in terms of
social and psychological characteristics, and who are the "next most
likely" to begin to engage in the crime. The ecological approach to
the problem of deterrence would be most effective if it could consider
the impact of sanctions not on the population in toto, but on the marginal group who are most vulnerable to involvement in the behavior.
The more specifically the marginal group can be defined and measured,
the more valid will be the conclusions regarding the efficacy of sanctions in changing criminal behaviors.

Areal Distributions and Homogeneous
Units of Analysis

Any research employing an ecological approach must take into
account the general problems of working with aggregate data (Taylor,

1968) as well as the specific problems involved in aggregating data
from areal distributions (Blalock, 1971). The units of analysis availabl
usually involve geographic regions, states, cities, and census tracts.
The dilemma stems from the inverse correlation between the size and
the homogeneity of units. Generally speaking, as the size of the unit
increases, the homogeneity of social characteristics within that unit
decreases (Cartwright, 1969:184). Thus, cities are more homogeneous
than states, and individual census tracts are more homogeneous than
a city as a whole. Occassionally, even relatively small units of analysis such as neighborhoods can be heterogeneous enough to produce
significant distortions in the data generated (Morris, 1958). Researchers using the ecological approach to the study of general deterrence
might be able to resolve this problem in large part by utilizing the
methodologies developed by ecologists for the identification of homogeneous sociological areal units. At least three such techniques are
available but have yet to be applied by sociologists to this problem:
the development of typologies based on social indicators (Tryon, 1955
and 1967; Shevky and Bell, 1955); the definition of natural crime areas
(Schmid, 1960b); and the use of isoplethic mapping (Hoiberg and Cloyd,
1971).

The first alternative involves the development of typologies to
define socially homogeneous sub-areas within a city. Tryon uses
cluster analysis of several measures of housing and population variables within census tracts, and develops three major measures of
family life, assimilation, and socioeconomic independence (Cartwright,
1969; Schmid, 1960b). Shevky considers social rank, urbanization and
segregation to reflect dimensions of social change, and selects appropriate available measures of each dimension to score census tracts.
Although their procedures differ, "similar dimensions of the Tryon
and the Shevky typologies are significantly correlated" (Schmid,
1960b:670).

The second alternative involves the selection of natural crime
areas within a city. Schmid (1960b) uses factor analysis to compare
the social characteristics of census tracts with known crime rates,
and thereby is able to delineate specific natural crime areas.

The most promising attempt to establish a methodology for the
identification of homogeneous social areas has been isoplethic mapping
Hoiberg and Cloyd (1971) note that most attempts to search for homogeneous social units begin with specific bounded units, such as census
tracts, which are heterogeneous in nature, and which are usually fixed
by relatively arbitary boundary lines. They argue that the resulting
distortion may be avoided by methods which "relate one social dimension to the territory at a time, and which relate this directly, without
the intervention of bounded territorial units" (1971:66). They demonstrate their procedure by drawing lines or isolines around homogeneou

18

areas which enclose the ecological distribution of homogeneous social status within a community setting. Such a technique is consistent with the sociological concepts of community and subculture, but allows the boundaries of communities and subcultural areas to be drawn with a precision never before possible. The use of isoplethic mapping, although relatively expensive and time-consuming, would guarantee a much greater homogeneity of the basic units of analysis in ecological studies than can possibly be achieved using such crude and relatively heterogeneous units as states or census tracts.

Summary and Conclusions

The ecological approach to the study of general deterrence has the potential to make a very significant contribution to the exploration and application of the concept. However, as it is presently being used, the conclusions suggested by ecological studies are at best tentative. Four specific suggestions have been made for the improvement of this potentially fruitful line of research. First, to insure that what is being examined is general deterrence, rather than specific deterrence, crime rates should be based only on the crimes of first offenders, rather than on those of both first offenders and recidivists. Second, to account for the fact that the effect of sanctions on the general public cannot be expected to be immediately visible after changes in official sanctions, research methodologies should be structured to allow for an appropriate time lag between cause and effect. Third, to avoid distortion in estimating the effectiveness of sanctions in changing behavior, the base line "population at risk" should be defined as specifically as possible, with the minimum requirement that all crime rates at least be calculated in terms of only the adult population. Fourth, and finally, to make valid estimates of the effect of sanctions, the unit of analysis being considered should be as homogeneous as possible. The homogeneity can be greatly improved by abandoning the large and arbitrary units of analysis presently used, such as whole states, cities or census tracts, in favor of small natural social areas, such as those derived from isoplethic mapping.

References

Andeneas, Johannes
   1966   The general preventive effects of punishment. University of Pennsylvania Law Review, 114: 949-83.

Bailey, W. C., L. N. Gray, and J. D. Martin
1970   Models of deterrence. Paper presented to American Socio-
        logical Association, Washington, D. C.

Bean, F. D., and R. G. Cushing
1971   Criminal homicide, punishment, and deterrence: Method-
        ological and substantive reconsiderations. Social Science
        Quarterly, 52: 267-89.

Blalock, Hubert M.
1971   Aggregation and measurement error. Social Forces, 50(De-
        cember): 151-65.

Cartwright, D. S.
1969   Ecological variables. In E. F. Borgatta (ed.), Sociological
        Methodology. San Francisco: Jossey-Bass.

Chiricos, T. G., and G. P. Waldo
1970   Punishments and crime: An examination of some empirical
        evidence. Social Problems, 18: 200-17.

Gibbs, J. P.
1968   Crime, punishment, and deterrence. Social Science Quar-
        terly, 48: 515-30.

Gray, L. N., and J. D. Martin
1969   Punishment and deterrence: Another analysis of Gibbs'
        data. Social Science Quarterly, 50: 389-95.

Hawkins, G.
1971   Punishment and deterrence: The educative, moralizing,
        and habituative effects. In S. E. Grupp (ed.), Theories of
        Punishment. Bloomington, Ind.: Indiana University Press.

Hoiberg, E. O., and J. S. Cloyd
1971   Definition and measurement of continuous variation in
        ecological analysis. American Sociological Review, 36:
        65-74.

Martin, J. D., and L. N. Gray
1971   Measurement of relative variation: Sociological examples.
        American Sociological Review, 36: 486-502.

Morris, T.
1958   The Criminal Area. London: Routledge and Kegan Paul.

Schmid, C.
  1960a Urban crime areas: Part I. American Sociological Review,
          25: 527-49.
  1960b Urban crime areas: Part II. Ibid., 25: 655-78.

Schwartz, B.
  1968 The effect in Philadelphia of Pennsylvania's increased pen-
        alties for rape and attempted rape. Journal of Criminal
        Law, Criminology and Police Science, 59: 509-15.

Shevky, E., and W. Bell
  1955 Social Area Analysis: Theory, Illustrative Applications
        and Computational Procedure. Stanford: Stanford University
        Press.

Taylor, C. L.
  1968 Aggregate Data Analysis. Paris: Mouton.

Teevan, J. J.
  1972 Deterrent effects of punishment: The Canadian case. Cana-
        dian Journal of Corrections, 14(January): 68-82.

Tittle, C. R.
  1969 Crime rates and legal sanctions. Social Problems, 16: 409-
        23.

Tryon, R. C.
  1955 The Identification of Social Areas by Cluster Analysis.
        Berkeley: University of California Press.
  1967 Predicting group differences in cluster analysis: The social
        area problem. Multivariate Behavioural Research, 2: 453-
        75.

Wilkins, L. T.
  1969 Evaluation of Penal Measures. New York: Random.

Zimring, F., and G. Hawkins
  1968 Deterrence and marginal groups. Journal of Research in
        Crime and Delinquency, 5(July): 100-14.

3

A CAUSAL FRAMEWORK
FOR THE ANALYSIS
OF DETERRENCE AND
RELATED PROCESSES
William J. Bowers

Retribution once served as the primary justification for the criminal sanction and dictated the form that such punishment should take. However, it has since fallen into disrepute on the grounds that it promotes excessively brutal forms of punishment and that it appeals to base human instincts. Deterrence has taken its place in the modern world as a more rational and humane basis for the criminal sanction (Packer, 1968).

Yet, among the legal punishments presently imposed for serious criminal offenses, there is virtually no evidence that one has greater deterrent power than another. The long tradition of research on capital punishment has consistently shown that the death penalty has no marginal deterrent effects over other sanctions imposed as alternatives.[1] More recent studies of certainty and severity of imprisonment have also failed to turn up evidence of marginal deterrence.[2] Thus deterrence, as a justification for criminal sanctions as they presently exist, may be a myth.[3]

In view of these negative results, perhaps the criminal sanction has served some other functions. Consider the following possibilities: (1) It may relieve public anxiety about high or rising crime rates if

---

A distinction is commonly made between the presumed power of criminal sanctions to prevent offenses (1) among past offenders on whom such punishments have been imposed (specific deterrence), and (2) among potential offenders who are more or less aware that such punishments are apt to be imposed (general deterrence). In the ensuing discussion, I will be using the term "deterrence" in the second sense, referring to general deterrence, unless I explicitly indicate otherwise.

the public believes in its deterrent power and authorities use it as if it were a deterrent. (2) It may satisfy deep-seated public needs for retribution if it is used disproportionately against those whose transgressions are particularly offensive to the public conscience. (3) It may reflect and reinforce social distinctions in the interests of the dominant or majority group against minorities. What evidence is there of these alternative functions or effects, and what implications do they have for the analysis of deterrence?

Repressive Response. If severe and certain punishment is perceived as an effective instrument for reducing the incidence of criminal behavior, one might expect to see "crackdowns" by the police and the "exemplary" use of legal punishment by the courts in the face of high or rising crime rates. Specifically, judges can be expected "to throw the book" at an offender in an effort to "curb the rising tide of crime," as a kind of "repressive response" to prior levels of or trends in the crime rate. Indeed, recent research showing more positive than negative correlations between crime rates and punishment levels for most offenses (Chiricos and Waldo, 1970) suggests that the criminal sanction may be serving as a repressive but ineffective response to crime. Research also indicates that the severity of formal sanctions imposed for excessive drinking behavior in college is a repressive but ineffective response to the levels of such misconduct occurring prior to the imposition of these sanctions (Bowers and Salem, 1972).

Retribution. This implies that legal sanctions be punitive rather than theraputic, and that the most punitive sanctions be imposed for the most serious or most disapproved transgressions against society. The widely documented failure of our penal system to rehabilitate (Martinson et al., 1972), is evidence of the punitive character of the criminal sanction. Research also shows that the duration of imprisonment imposed for various categories of crimes closely follows public judgments of the seriousness of these offenses (Sellin and Wolfgang, 1964). Furthermore, research on college students reveals that more severe punishments will be imposed for a given offense on campuses where disapproval of that behavior is more intense (Salem and Bowers, 1968). Thus, society appears to have a relatively strict rule of retribution requiring more punitive sanctions for more serious offenses.

Minority group oppression. That the criminal sanction is used in a discriminatory fashion against blacks and the poor has been well documented in studies of decisions by the police about the disposition of juveniles who have been apprehended of provision of counsel to defendants (Sutherland and Cressey, 1966), in commitment to prison (Korn and McCorkle, 1959), in length of sentence imposed (Korn and McCorkle, 1959) and in the imposition of the death penalty (Bowers, 1972a). The data on capital punishment suggests that these differences in treatment of minority groups may reflect efforts on the part of the dominant majority to keep the minority "in its place." They show that racial discrimination in capital punishment had been much more pronounced over an extended period of time in the South than in the rest of the United States.

In effect, then, legal punishment may be a function of prior levels of or trends in crime, of community characteristics such as public sentiments of disapproval, and of characteristics of offenders such as race and social class. At the same time factors such as race, social class, and community norms have also been identified as important determinants of crime. Thus, it would appear that crime and punishment may share common roots and have reciprocal effects— obviously complicating the assessment of mechanisms such as deterrence.

By focusing narrowly on punishment as a determinant of crime rates, the general deterrence perspective has tended to obscure the more complex causal interrelationships between crime and punishment in society, and to overlook confounding factors in evaluating deterrent effects. My purpose here will be to develop a more causal model of the various relationships between crime and punishment that provides for the assessment of these relationships independently and in relation to one another.

The Causal Framework

Sociologists have recently begun to apply techniques of causal modeling in the analysis of social processes. Originally developed in biology (Wright, 1960) and refined by economists (Johnson, 1963; Goldberger, 1964), these techniques have been introduced to sociologists in the work of Blalock (1961 and later) and Duncan (1966) and their application is perhaps best illustrated in work on the American occupational structure (Blau and Duncan, 1967). I suggest how these techniques may be applied in the analysis of the complex relationship between crime and punishment in society.

Two components of a general causal model of the crime-punishment relationship can be distinguished: (1) causal links between crime and punishment, and (2) the causal context of crime and punishment. These two components permit the operationalization of various concepts, including deterrence, repressive response, retribution, and minority group oppression, and illustrate how the application of this general model will help to overcome methodological problems in previous research on deterrence.

I. Causal links between crime and punishment— the problem of offsetting effects

The concept of deterrence essentially refers to the causal impact that punishment is supposed to have on deviant or criminal behavior. Greater certainty, severity, or celerity of punishment should, according to the deterrence perspective, reduce the incidence of criminal behavior by increasing the risks of the potential offender (direct effects) and by strengthening commitment to the law (educative or moralizing effects) in broader society (Andenaes, 1952, 1966; Zimring, 1971).

A causal link between crime and punishment is equally inherent in the concept of repressive response. While the judge who "throws the book" at an offender in order to "curb the rising tide of crime" may be acting on the belief that it will have a deterrent effect, his action explicitly illustrates how prior fluctuations in the crime rate may have a direct causal impact on the legal punishments subsequently imposed. His action is obviously a direct consequence of prior levels of or trends in criminal behavior.

The simultaneous operation of both general deterrence and repressive response effects has a very important implication: namely, that the assessment of either effect is apt to be confounded in cross-sectional data. Thus, repressive response will tend to produce a positive association between crime and punishment at a given point in time (e.g., more crime leads to more severe punishment); deterrent effects will tend to yield a negative association between the two at the same time (e.g., more severe punishment leads to less crime). For an adequate assessment of both deterrent and repressive response, then, one must be able to separate these two potentially offsetting effects. This requires measures of crime and punishment over time, and control for prior levels of these variables in assessing the effects of one on the other.

The model in Figure 3.1 represents this situation. It shows crime and punishment at two points in time (t and t-1) and, by means of arrows, it represents the effects of prior crime rates (C_{t-1}) on later crime and punishment (C_t and S_t), the effects of prior punishment (S_{t-1}) on later crime and punishment (again C_t and S_t), and the correlation between prior crime and punishment levels (represented by the double-headed arrows connecting S_{t-1} and C_{t-1}.) In effect, the model transforms or decomposes the correlation between crime and punishment at a given point in time (between C_t and S_t) into four causal links and one unanalyzed correlation.

Notably, negative general deterrence effects (GD) and positive repressive response (RR), which would be confounded in cross-sectional data, are now distinguishable. The assessment of deterrence

FIGURE 3.1

Model of Direct Causal Connections
Between Crime and Punishment

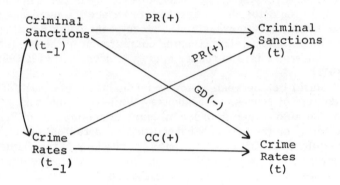

Identification of effect parameters
Leading to Criminal Sanctions (t)
PR = Precedent
RR = Repressive Response
Leading to Crime Rates (t)
GD = General Deterrence
CC = Crime Constancy

(the GD parameter) is made <u>controlling</u> for the effects of prior offense levels; the assessment of repressive response (the RR parameter) is made controlling for effects of prior sanctioning levels. The precedent (PR) and crime consistency (CC) parameters reflect the extent to which crime and punishment are a function of relatively stable, long-term characteristics of the aggregate that serves as the unit of analysis, and the degree to which individual factors are cancelled out in the aggregation process.

While the model in Figure 3.1 is sufficient to convey the problem of offsetting effects, with some simple refinements it can be used to identify additional issues in the analysis of causal links between crime and punishment. The following modifications are proposed: (1) adding prior trends in crime and punishment to the absolute levels of these variables, (2) incorporating various types of offenses into the same model, (3) disaggregating total crime and punishment indices into subgroup specific rates and trends, and (4) applying the model selectively by social context and type of offense.

26

Prior trends in crime and punishment. This discussion has incorporated the notion that prior trends, as well as absolute levels, of crime and punishment may account for subsequent levels of these variables. Thus, for example, to the degree that those who impose punishments judge the seriousness of the problem by the change it represents from prior conditions, rising rather than high crime rates are apt to provoke a repressive response. By the same token, to the extent that social action is affected by the patterning or scheduling of rewards and punishments, as learning theory would suggest, it is likely that trends in, as opposed to the absolute levels of, punishment will affect subsequent criminal behavior.

Various offenses incorporated in the same model. By including data on the rates and trends in crime and punishment for several different offenses in the same model, it becomes possible to distinguish among particularized, generalized, and selective forms of deterrence and repressive response. With respect to deterrence, for example, increased punishment for a given offense may lead to the reduced incidence of that behavior and only that behavior (the classical case referred to as particularized deterrence); increased punishment for a given offense may, however, lead to the reduced incidence of several forms of criminal activity, reflecting generalized deterrence; and increased punishment for a given offense may lead to the reduced incidence of a different offense, representing selective deterrence. Following the same logic, one can distinguish among particularized, generalized, and selective forms of repressive response. The centralized nature of state law enforcement and judicial machinery suggests the possibility of generalized repressive response, and the public's vague awareness of criminal sanctioning practices (California State Legislature, 1968) point to the possibility of selective or generalized deterrence.

Subgroup specific levels and trends in crime and punishment. By replacing aggregate crime and punishment rates and trends with subgroup indices, it becomes possible to identify differentials, discrimination and displacement in deterrence and repressive response effects. Thus, for example, by estimating repressive response parameters for both whites and nonwhites, it would be possible to determine whether high or rising crime rates provoke equally severe criminal sanctions against offenders of both races. This might reveal evidence of discriminatory repressive response against Negroes. Similarly, punishment may not have a uniform effect on crime rates for both groups. As a socially marginal group, Negroes may be less subject to whatever deterrent power criminal sanctions have. Hence, there may be differential deterrent effects (among nonwhites only).

Another possibility is that levels of crime within one population subgroup may affect the punishments imposed on members of another subgroup, producing what might be referred to as <u>displaced</u> repressive response. Or again, severe sanctions imposed on one subgroup may have deterrent effects on subsequent crime rates of another subgroup, indicating <u>displaced</u> deterrence.

   <u>Selective application by social context and type of offense</u>. Evidence of deterrence and repressive response, and particularly patterns of selectivity, displacement, and discrimination in these effects, may vary by social context and type of offense. For example, discriminatory repressive response against Negroes may be more pronounced in the regional context of the South where a racial caste system has been institutionalized for many years. This pattern may also be more pronounced with respect to crimes of interpersonal violence which may tend to provoke fear and hostility toward racial and ethnic minorities in society.

   Each of these modifications of the model in Figure 3.1 could be presented in more detail. Although here considered separately for the most part, they could be represented in more elaborate versions of Figure 3.1.

II. <u>The causal context of crime and punishment</u>:
<u>The problem of spuriousness</u>

   Apart from causal links between crime and punishment, the crime-punishment relationship in society may have another source; namely, the possibility that both crime and punishment share <u>common</u> causes. In the long history of efforts to identify the roots of criminal behavior, the following major sources of crime have emerged: (1) <u>Social disorganization</u> seen in the generally higher crime rates in industrialized and urbanized areas, particularly the disoriented urban slum; (2) <u>social deprivation</u> evident in the higher crime rates among the poor, badly educated and unemployed; (3) intergroup conflict manifested in the higher crime rates among blacks as of late, and among successive immigrant groups, the Irish, Italian, and Jews before them; and (4) cultural values toward persons and property reflected in variation in crime rates by region, religious orientation, and educational level of the community.

   Suppose that these same social factors also affect the punishments the community imposes for criminal behavior. Thus, the socially disorganized community may have difficulty identifying and apprehending offenders, the socially deprived community may lack enforcement resources, where intergroup conflict prevails criminal sanctions may be used as a harsh instrument of minority group oppression, and where cultural values and norms are strongly held punishments may be strictly imposed. In other words, common causes of crime and punishment may be responsible for an association between the two which is not due to causal links between them.

To correctly assess the causal connections between crime and punishment, then, one must take account of these possible sources of spuriousness. Consequently, the model of the causal context of crime and punishment presented in Figure 3.2 shows social factors contributing to <u>both</u> crime <u>and</u> punishment. A description of each factor's presumed effects on both crime and punishment illustrates how the relationship between crime and punishment may be affected by the causes they share.

Social disorganization. Common indicators of social disorganization include population density, industrialization, urban concentration, residential mobility and family instability. These conditions of social disorganization are supposed to be linked to criminal behavior through the development of an illicit opportunity structure providing differential association with criminal elements. Hence, the path from social disorganization to crime rates in Figure 3.2 is labeled "illicit opportunity structures." On the other hand, the effect of social disorganization on criminal sanctions may be to reduce the certainty of legal punishment through the high anonymity and low observability of behavior in socially disorganized settings. Thus, I have labeled the path from social disorganization to criminal sanctions "anonymity/observability."

Social deprivation. Low levels of income, education, and employment are indicative of social deprivation. The extent to which such conditions are concentrated in population subgroups reflects the "relative deprivation" of that subgroup. Conditions of absolute and particularly relative deprivation are thought to produce criminal behavior, by causing the deprived to reject the legitimate opportunities or means for achieving success in society—hence the label "delegitimation of socially prescribed means." Social deprivation may affect the legal sanctions imposed for crime via the resources available for enforcement and corrections. Since it is expressive to apprehend and imprison offenders, the socially deprived community cannot be expected to commit extensive "enforcement resources" to these tasks, and hence both the certainty and severity of legal punishments are apt to be relatively low.

Intergroup conflict. The presence of racial and ethnic minorities and their position in the community reflect a potential for intergroup tensions and conflict; and differentials in education, income, and employment, between minority and majority group members suggest the presence of racial or ethnic discrimination. Intergroup conflict is supposed to contribute to the frustration, aggression, and hostility toward outsiders which such conditions tend to generate. I have therefore labeled this effect "aggression/hostility." The criminal sanction, under conditions of intergroup tension and conflict, may become an instrument of "minority group oppression." In the hands of the majority it may become a tool for keeping minorities "in their place."

29

FIGURE 3.2

Model of the Causal Context of Crime and Punishment

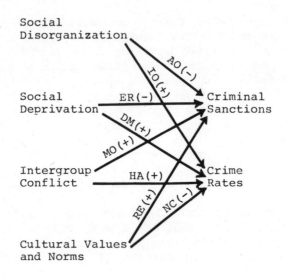

Identification of effect parameters

    Leading to Criminal Sanctions

        AO = Anonymity/observability
        ER = Enforcement Resources
        MO = Minority Group Oppression
        RE = Retribution

    Leading to Crime Rates

        IO = Illicit Opportunity Structures
        DM = Delegitimation of Socially Prescribed Means
        HA = Other Directed Hostility and Aggression
        NC = Informal Normative Constraints

Cultural values. General values and norms toward persons and property are undoubtedly rooted in the fundamental social conditions and the broader cultural heritage of the community—religious, political and regional factors. The normative climate of the community or its condemnation of criminality will tend to have a constraining effect on criminal behavior. I have therefore labeled the path from cultural values to criminal bahavior as the "normative constraint" effect. At the same time, the normative climate or condemnation of criminality that prevails can also be expected to have an effect, especially on the severity of punishment imposed for crime. Indeed, the idea that the punishment should "fit the crime" is, of course, contingent on social definitions of what is appropriate or proper retribution. Thus, I have labeled the path from normative climate to criminal sanctions as the effect of "retribution."

Having outlined this working model of the causal context of the crime-punishment relationship, I am now in a position to illustrate the possibly misleading effects of these causal factors. Note, for example, in Figure 3.2, that social deprivation is presumed to contribute positively to crime rates via delegitimation of socially prescribed means (DM) and negatively to sanctioning practices via lack of enforcement resources (ER). Social deprivation will therefore tend to produce a negative correlation between crime and punishment apart from any causal link between the two. The same goes for social disorganization and cultural values, as indicated in Figure 3.2. Social disorganization contributes positively to crime rates and negatively to criminal sanctions. Thus, the operation of these three causal factors will, at least according to the assumptions represented in Figure 3.2, produce the kind of negative correlation between crime and punishment which has been mistakenly interpreted as evidence of deterrence.

By contrast, intergroup conflict and tension, according to Figure 2.2, is presumed to contribute positively to both crime and punishment—to crime rates via other-directed hostility and aggression (HA) and to criminal sanction via minority group oppression (MO). Intergroup conflict will therefore tend to produce a positive correlation between crime and punishment again apart from any causal connection between the two. Moreover, the effects of intergroup conflict will offset those of the other three causal factors, tending to reduce the negative correlation between crime and punishment that they would produce (while at the same time adding to the accounted for variation in crime and punishment). Hence, the likelihood that crime and punishment are products of the same social factors is not necessarily revealed by the strength of the correlation between the two. Relatively low and inconsistent correlations between them may mean only that the causes they share are having offsetting effects—in the same way

31

that repressive response and general deterrence effects may obscure one another.

III. Some implications of combining the two components

With long-term time series data, it would become possible to examine crime and punishment for their effects on social disorganization, social deprivation, intergroup conflict, and cultural values—which in turn affect crime and punishment. It could be that high or rising levels of violent crime over an extended period of time will cause high-status members of the community to move out, thereby increasing the level of social deprivation which in turn leads to still higher crime rates. This suggests a "vicious cycle of spiraling crime rates."

Alternatively, rising crime rates at an earlier point in time (though perhaps not over an extended period of time) may stimulate or activate the normative climate of the community, thus curbing the rising crime rates via stronger informal constraints and strengthening the punishments imposed via stronger retributive effects. This latter effect represents a form of repressive response (i.e., positive association between prior crime rates and subsequent punishment)—one which may be termed "delayed" repressive response, since it occurs over a relatively long period and indirectly through the changes brought about in the normative sentiments of the community.

Or again, high or rising levels of punishment, especially if they are applied in a discriminatory fashion, could conceivably produce out-migration among minority group members. This would eventually lower the level of intergroup conflict in the community and hence lower the subsequent crime rates, thus producing what might be termed deterrence by attrition. That is, aside from the fear it is supposed to evoke in potential offenders and its presumed moralizing or educative qualities, punishment may have a deterrent effect through its impact on the population composition of the community.

Still further elaborations and extensions of the basic model may prove useful. It may be, for instance, that violence against persons causes out-migration among high status community members and hence greater social deprivation; whereas, property offenses may tend to activate the normative climate, producing stronger informal normative constraints and more emphasis on retribution. Having indices of both kinds of offenses in the same model would obviously improve the ability to understand such complex processes.

Conclusion

The application of the general causal model presented here can improve an understanding of the complex relationship between crime and punishment in society. In addition to possible deterrence effects, one must evaluate other functions of the criminal sanction, including repressive response, retribution, and minority group oppression. This model explicitly operationalizes these and other functions and effects of the criminal sanction. Its application may lead to a reappraisal of the role of the criminal sanction in society.

Moreover, the model offers an advantage in the evaluation of deterrent effects. Previous studies attempting to control for or remove spuriousness and offsetting effects have done so without specifically identifying the factors responsible for them. This has caused controls to be imprecise and research designs to be restricted in scope. And, of course, it has tended to obscure rather than explicate the causal context of and connections between crime and punishment.

A thoroughgoing application of this model requires extended time series data on crime, punishment, and community characteristics. Available data on homicide and capital punishment at the state level in the United States meets this requirement. Demographic characteristics of states are readily available from census publications. Homicide rates by states are published annually by the FBI. Annual data on executions by states at least since 1930 is available from the Federal Bureau of Prisons.

Data on the likelihood and duration of imprisonment for various offenses has also been published by the Federal Bureau of Prisons, but not continuously and not over an extended period of time. No doubt, other data exists, perhaps at the level of counties or cities, which has been collected for research purposes or as a matter of official record-keeping, that would be especially suitable for the application of this model. California, Illinois, and New York may have such data as a result of efforts to develop more systematic and comprehensive information on their criminal justice systems.

Furthermore, data at these lower levels of aggregation may reveal the operation of deterrence or repressive response effects which take place on a relatively local level and are not detectable in larger aggregates. Obviously, the use of victimization surveys to validate and adjust for biases in police-reported crime rates would be valuable. They could also be used to supplement demographic information, especially for the measurement of complex causal factors such as intergroup conflict or the prominence of a "subculture of violence" in the community.

Finally, the development and application of models such as this one point to the need for better crime-reporting techniques and for more generally available data banks on the operation of the criminal justice system. Where data of this sort is routinely available, it would be possible to have an ongoing evaluation of the criminal sanction—the effects it is having and the functions it is serving at various times and locations in society.

Notes

1. The inference that the death penalty had no marginal deterrent effects over punishments used as alternatives comes from a diverse collection of studies that compare homicide rates (1) for neighboring countries and contiguous states of the United States with and without the death penalty (Scheussler, 1952; United Nations, 1962); (2) before and after the abolition of capital punishment and its reinstatement in states which have made such changes (Scheussler, 1952; Sellin, 1967); and (3) before and after the imposition of the death sentence and the execution of convicted offenders in local communities (Dann, 1935; Savitz, 1958). While some critics have argued that this evidence is still "inconclusive" (Gibbs, 1968: 516) or that it does not "disprove" the operation of deterrent effects (Van den Haag, 1969), the conspicuous and consistent absence of such effects in the various studies puts critics in a difficult position (see Bedau, 1970, 1971). As Chambliss (1967: 706) notes: "Given the preponderance of evidence, it seems safe to conclude that capital punishment does not act as an effective deterrent to murder."

2. Research by Gibbs (1968) suggested that certainty and severity of imprisonment for homicide lead to lower rates of homicide. Shortly thereafter, Tittle (1969) reported that Gibbs' certainty effect held up for assault, robbery, burglary, larceny, auto theft and sex offenses, as well as homicide; but that his severity effects could not be generalized to other offenses. Yet this limited support for deterrence could not withstand critical scrutiny. Chiricos and Waldo (1970) have shown that Tittle's certainty effects are artifactual; they derive from a built-in correlation between his measures of certainty and offense rates, and they can be reproduced with random data. Furthermore, Bowers (1972b) has shown that Gibbs' findings are also misleading by demonstrating (1) that both severity and certainty measures used by Gibbs are a function of prior variations in the homicide rate, and (2) that the reported deterrent effects of severity and certainty of imprisonment disappear when he controls for region of the country (Zimring, 1971, has also noted this second point).

3. I do not mean to imply that rewards and punishments have no effect on human behavior, or more particularly, the punishment does not deter deviant behavior. Indeed, some evidence of deterrence

has been uncovered. There is some evidence of general deterrence in the case of parking violations (Chambliss, 1966), speeding violations (Ross and Campbell, 1968), and income tax fraud (Schwartz and Orleans, 1967; Schwartz, 1969). The threat of disclosure (but not the fact of it) for someone who is otherwise leading a conventional existence, as in the case of amateur shoplifting (Cameron, 1967), appears to have specific deterrent effects. Thus, where the action is goal-directed, where the risk and cost of nonconformity can be accurately calculated as in monetary terms, and where the pool of potential offenders includes virtually everyone, particularly people leading "straight lives," formal punishment and/or the threat of it, may be a deterrent (cf. Andeneas, 1952, 1971). Where the actions are expressive of a particularly lifestyle, characteristics of a subculture, or confined to a population subgroup, which may be true of major criminal offenses, formal punishment would appear to have little effect on behavior (cf. Chambliss, 1966, 1967).

References

Andeneas, Johannes
  1952   General prevention: Illusion or reality? Journal of Criminal Law, Criminology and Police Science, 176: 181-90.
  1966   The general preventive effects of punishment. University of Pennsylvania Law Review, 114: 949.
  1971   Deterrence and specific offences. University of Chicago Law Review, 38: 537-53.

Bedau, Hugo Adam
  1970   The death penalty as a deterrent: Argument and evidence. Ethics, 80: 205-17.
  1971   Deterrence and the death penalty: A reconsideration. Journal of Criminal Law, Criminology and Police Science, 61: 539-48.

Blalock, Hubert M., Jr.
  1961   Causal Inference in Non-Experimental Research. Chapel Hill, N.C.: University of North Carolina Press.

Blau, Peter M., and O. D. Duncan
  1967   The American Occupational Structure. New York: Wiley.

Bowers, William J.
  1972a   Racial Discrimination in Capital Punishment. Lexington, Mass.: Lexington Books.

1972b   Repression, retribution, and deterrence: A working paper. Boston, Mass.: Center for Applied Social Research, Northeastern University.

Bowers, William J., and Richard Salem
1972   Severity of formal sanctions as a repressive response to deviant behavior. Law and Society Review, 7: 427-41.

California State Legislature
1968   Deterrent effects of criminal sanctions. Progress report of the Assembly Committee on Criminal Procedure.

Cameron, Mary
1964   The Booster and the Snitch. New York: Free Press.

Chambliss, William J.
1966   The deterrent influence of punishment. Crime and Delinquency, 12: 70-75.
1967   Types of deviance and the effectiveness of legal sanctions. University of Wisconsin Law Review, Summer #3: 703-19.

Chiricos, Theodore G., and Gordon P. Waldo
1970   Punishment and crime: An examination of some empirical evidence. Social Problems, 18: 200-17.

Dann, Robert H.
1935   The deterrent effect of capital punishment. The Committee of Philanthropic Labor of Philadelphia, Yearly Meeting of Friends, Bulletin No. 32.

Duncan, O. D.
1966   Path analysis: Some sociological examples. American Journal of Sociology, 72: 1-16.

Gibbs, Jack P.
1968   Crime, punishment and deterrence. Southwestern Social Science Quarterly, 48: 515-30.

Goldberger, Arthur S.
1964   Economic Theory. New York: Wiley.

Johnson, J.
1963   Econometric methods. New York: McGraw-Hill.

Korn, Richard, and Lloyd McCorkle
1959   Criminology and penology. New York: Holt, Rinehart and
        Winston.

Martinson, Robert, et al.
1972   The Treatment Evaluation Survey. New York: Office of
        Crime Control Planning, State of New York.

Packer, Herbert L.
1968   The Limits of the Criminal Sanction. Stanford: Stanford
        University Press.

Ross, H. Laurence, and Donald T. Campbell
1968   The Connecticut speed crackdown. In H. Laurence Ross
        (ed.), Perspectives on the Social Order. New York: Mc-
        Graw-Hill.

Salem, Richard G., and William J. Bowers
1968   Severity of formal sanctions as a deterrent to deviant be-
        havior. Law and Society Review, 5: 21-40.

Savitz, Leonard
1958   A study of capital punishment. Journal of Criminal Law,
        Criminology and Police Science, 49: 338-41.

Scheussler, Karl
1952   The deterrent influence of the death penalty. Annals of the
        American Academy of Political and Social Science, 284:
        54-62.

Schwartz, Richard F.
1969   Sanctions and compliance. Paper presented at meeting of
        American Sociological Association, San Francisco.

Schwartz, Richard F., and S. Orleans
1967   On legal sanctions. University of Chicago Law Review, 34:
        274-300.

Sellin, Thorsten
1967   Capital Punishment. New York: Harper and Row.

Sellin, Thorsten, and Marvin E. Wolfgang
1964   The Measurement of Delinquency. New York: Wiley.

Sutherland, Edwin H., and Donald R. Cressey
   1966   Principles of Criminology. 7th ed., Philadelphia: Lippincott.

Tittle, Charles R.
   1969   Crimes rates and legal sanctions. Social Problems, 16: 409-23.

United Nations
   1962   Capital Punishment. New York: United Nations.

Van den Haag, Ernest
   1969   On deterrence and the death penalty. Journal of Criminal Law, Criminology and Police Science, 60: 141-47.

Wright, Sewall
   1960   Path coefficients and path regressions. Biometrics, 16: 189-202.

Zimring, Franklin E.
   1971   Perspectives on Deterrence. National Institute of Mental Health, Public Health Service Publication 2056.

4

DETERRENCE AND THE
MARIHUANA SMOKER
Stanley E. Grupp

There is wide agreement today that the control procedures for dealing with the marihuana problem (and drug abuse in the wider sense) are in a state of disarray, characterized not only by inconsistency in arrest procedures and in the decision to prosecute, but by general disagreement regarding what the objectives really are. In the effort to reach consensus and to resolve ambivalencies, it is imperative that attention not only be given to the question of criminal sanctions or no criminal sanctions, but to the empirical question of whether or not one can in fact control marihuana use through use of the criminal law and if so, the circumstances required to achieve this objective: who can be controlled, under what circumstances, and whether the price is worth it. Critics of the criminal sanction approach assert either that marihuana consumption cannot be deterred, or that in view of the widespread use of marihuana and its innocuous effects, it is not worth the cost. It is not hard to demonstrate, for example, that much of the police activity in making cases against marihuana sellers and consumers is for nought: State's Attorneys commonly fail to prosecute, and when they do, they often accept negotiated pleas to substantially reduced charges. Available evidence also indicates that the sentencing trend itself for the few cases that reach this stage has been one of increasing amelioration in recent years (Grupp and Lucas, 1970; Grupp, 1971). These features, together with the growing social acceptance of marihuana, mitigate against investigations aimed at examining the question of the deterrability of marihuana consumers.

Reprinted by permission of the publisher from The Marihuana Muddle by Stanley E. Grupp (Lexington, Mass.: Lexington Books, D.C. Heath and Company, 1973), pp. 169-77.

The research for this paper was supported in part by MH 14157, MH 17196, and by Illinois State University Grant 71-5.

Marihuana smoking per se is typically a casual, noncompulsive phenomenon. Most smokers can take it or leave it, depending on their disposition and the circumstances. Consistent with this point of view, it has been argued elsewhere that the demand for marihuana is elastic; that is, it is responsive to changes that occur in the quantity of available marihuana (Grupp and Koch, 1971). This line of reasoning suggests that the amount of marihuana consumed can be reduced by tying up the distribution channels, either by taking the sellers out of the market through use of the criminal sanction, or by destroying the marihuana-growing fields. In a broad sense these features are evidence of the potential for a viable deterrent strategy in the control of marihuana. It must be frankly admitted, however, that since many established marihuana smokers often find themselves in the position of seller or dealer, the prospect for completely eliminating the seller from the market is not a realistic objective. A complete test of the classical deterrent ideal is thought of as requiring certain and rapid detection and consistent punishment. Some of these prerequisites may not be possible; for others, American society today is not prepared to pay the price. Short of the classical conditions necessary to achieve the maximum deterrent effect, given the nature of the typical marihuana smoker's nonchalant attitude toward the use of marihuana and the accompanying elastic nature of the demand, it is possible nevertheless that some measure of deterrability can be achieved even in the face of the ethical problems of control, the unresolved ambivalencies regarding marihuana, and the vacillating control policies which emanate from this lack of specification.

In view of the considerable discussion about the abandonment of penal sanctions for the possession of small amounts of marihuana for personal use, some might argue that it is academic to inquire whether or not one can deter marihuana smoking. It remains a problematic issue, however, as to whether or not criminal sanctions will be eliminated. Regardless of the ultimate direction the criminal law takes in this area, the problem of control of marihuana will continue to confront the society. There will be a continued discouragement of persons from becoming daily, regular and habitual users. It will probably continue to be assumed that the sale of marihuana and possession of relatively large amounts can be controlled through the use of criminal sanctions. The question of control of marihuana use and sale is not, therefore, merely an academic issue. It is a question which will continue to harass Americans for a long time to come.

The sample used in generating the data for the present paper is particularly germane to the broader issue put in the above manner. It involves subjects who were extensively involved with marihuana; most of them had experience with other drugs; some were intensive users of a drug other than marihuana. Regardless of whether one admits the deterrent argument with respect to casual and occasional use of marihuana, these subjects represent the kind of drug-use patterns that will continue to be discouraged. Therefore, an examination of the applicability of the deterrent argument, the extent to which marihuana smokers are deterred, and variables associated with this event may provide useful hints about possible directions that control policies might take.

There is some indirect evidence, in addition to the argument involving the elasticity of the demand for marihuana, which indicates that the deterrent factor is operating in this area:

1. The very fact that there is so much concern about the ostensible severity and punitiveness of laws relevant to marihuana is indirect evidence that the law itself is a salient factor in many persons' minds. This concern is ongoing in spite of the fact, and this is widely known to marihuana smokers themselves, that relatively few of the persons who smoke marihuana are ever arrested and still fewer are actually convicted. This attrition continues through the adjudication process. In other words, the possibility of arrest, actual arrest, or the more remote chance of conviction is sufficient to cause some persons not only to be concerned but presumably to be governed or have their actions influenced to at least some extent.

2. There is one point that is almost always made, even by spokesmen who are critical of the existing laws regulating marihuana; namely that when you use or become involved with persons who use marihuana, you should be aware that this is prohibited by the criminal law and that by your actions you are vulnerable to arrest and prosecution. Thus, some people are expected to be guided by the fact of illegaility, either by refraining from the use of marihuana or by exercising greater discretion in the use of marihuana.

3. There is evidence of the deterrent factor at work in still other ways. Following police raids involving marihuana and other drug charges, the typical response in the university drug-using community is one of greater restraint and circumspection in the use of drugs.

These examples appear to mean that there is a deterrent factor operating apropos marihuana control by the police. This, of course, does not mean that behavior involving marihuana is the ideal type of behavior-circumstance for implementing the deterrent mechanism.[1] Clearly there is a need to gather more evidence regarding the conditions under which one can expect to maximize the returns from the application of the deterrent principle to the use and sale of marihuana.

Assuming that the deterrent mechanism operates with experienced smokers, it is interesting to determine whether this would be reflected in responses provided by a cross-section of 90 experienced marihuana smokers, and if so, what features, if any, appear to distinguish those marihuana smokers who give evidence of deterrability and those who do not.

Methodology

A <u>selected</u> sample of 90 established smokers was interviewed. Every effort was made to obtain marihuana smokers from various social strata. The final sample represents 53 blacks and 37 whites. Represented are 30 college students, primarily at Illinois State University; 30 prison inmates at the Pontiac branch of the Illinois Department of Corrections; and 30 blacks from the south side of Chicago.

Males dominated the sample, with 75 males and 15 female. Of the sample, 67 respondents were 21 years of age or younger; 70 were single and had never been married; 46 had finished high school, while 44 either had not finished or were still in high school.

Information was collected by means of a 27-page interview instrument. Interviews typically lasted from one hour to an hour and a half. Completed interviews were considered usable if (1) the subject had fairly intense experience with marihuana, (2) if he had <u>not</u> used heroin. Three persons retained in the sample had some experience with codeine cough syrup, and 4 had smoked opium. No others had any experiences with opiates. Intense experience with marihuana was based on an assessment of several variables, including the estimated number of times per week and the last time the individual smoked marihuana. All subjects had extensive experience with marihuana. A commanding proportion indicated they smoked two or more times a week and also has smoked within the previous week. Virtually all had smoked marihuana dozens of times. Where a recent time dimension was involved, the subjects who were imprisoned were asked to respond to the questions in terms of when they were last on the streets.

Several procedures were used to locate subjects. To locate college students and street blacks, information was spread by word-of-mouth and key informants were used to encourage marihuana smokers who they knew to make themselves available for interview. Prison inmates were screened from a list of names developed through a search of case files and those provided by prison sociologists.

Interviewing extended over a period of 19 months from June, 1968 through December, 1969. There is confidence that the sample does represent intensive marihuana smokers, and that no other procedure would produce a better sample of this type of smoker, but it is not known how representative the sample may be of the entire popula tion of marihuana smokers. It cannot be assumed, for example, that the data reflects the many persons with much less experience. Neither is the data necessarily reflective of all persons who have had extensive marihuana experience. While it is unfortunate that this is the case, it is a situation that occurs in investigations of this kind and a problem not easily rectified. It is felt that the broad range of subjects represented does in part compensate for these integral limitations.

Questions used in generating data on deterrence and used as the basis for analysis are:

1. "Have you ever turned down a chance to use marihuana because you thought you might be caught?"

2. "Do you think you will be smoking marihuana 10 years hence?"

3. "Did you try marihuana the first time you had an opportunity to do so?"

Responses on these questions are compared with innumerable social and drug patterns to determine what variables appear to distinguish the deterred and those not deterred. These variables include but are not limited to the usual demographic data, an extensive number of variables related to marihuana (for example, attitudes toward and initiation into smoking, friends' experience, projected experience), experiences with other drugs, anticipated experiences with other drugs, and a number of variables related to heroin (for example, attitude toward, friends' attitudes, knowledge of, opportunities to use, and the dimensions of the opportunity setting).[2]

Evidence of Deterrence

Fear of Being Caught. Interviewees were asked, "Have you ever turned down a chance to use marihuana because you thought you might be caught?" A positive response to this question is taken as clear evidence of the deterrent mechanism in operation. Of the 90 subjects, 37 said that there had been some occasion when they had turned down a chance to smoke marihuana because they were afraid of being caught.

Responses to an open-ended question which asked respondents to describe the circumstances in which they had been deterred are summarized in Table 4.1. It is apparent that where specific responses were given, the circumstances of abstention were of a deterrent nature. Subjects were afraid of being detected or of exposure, and restrained themselves accordingly.

The 37 deterred subjects offer an avenue and possibly valuable source of information regarding the deterrability of marihuana smoking and the categories of individuals who can be deterred. Statistically significant comparisons of those who have abstained from marihuana smoking because of fear of being caught and those who have not are presented in Table 4.2.

43

TABLE 4.1

Circumstances of Abstension from Smoking Marihuana Because of the Fear of Being Caught

Circumstances	Number of Subjects Mentioning
Police apt to be present or situation tight	11
Time or place not safe or right	11
With careless people	3
With untrustworthy people or persons you don't know	3
Afraid of being caught by friend or relative	2
When planning activity which is real visible	1
No specific circumstance mentioned	6

Who is most apt to fall in the deterrable category? It is not surprising that whites and college students are more apt to have experienced deterrence than their counterparts. One would expect that middle-class persons would be more apt to be subject to the socializing features of the criminal law and to middle-class values, which generally stigmatize marihuana smoking. It should be noted that the whites and college population were very comparable; there were only 7 whites in the entire sample who were not college students.

Subjects who had some experience with other drugs were more apt to fall in the deterrent category than those whose experience had been limited to marihuana. Specific experience with amphetamines was also associated with deterrability. Only 2 of the 17 exclusive marihuana smokers said that they had ever been restrained because of the fear of being caught. Subjects who on some occasion have experienced difficulty obtaining marihuana are more apt than their counterparts to have been deterred.

Projected Marihuana Experience Ten Years Hence. The question was asked, "Do you think you will be smoking marihuana 10 years from now?" A negative response, while not suggesting deterrence in the hedonistic calculus sense, does suggest that individuals anticipate that for some reason they will be restrained from smoking marihuana.

44

TABLE 4.2

Characteristics Associated with Having Turned
Down Chance to Smoke Marihuana Because of Fear of
Being Caught

| Characteristic | Fear of Being Caught* | |
	Yes	No
Race		
Black	16 (31)	36 (69)
White	21 (57)	16 (43)
	$X^2 = 4.99 < .05$	
Status		
College	17 (57)	13 (43)
Prison	13 (45)	16 (55)
Ghetto blacks	7 (23)	23 (77)
	$X^2 = 7.05 < .05$	
Some experience with a drug other than marihuana		
Yes	35 (49)	37 (51)
No	2 (12)	15 (88)
	$X^2 = 6.24 < .05$	
Experience with amphetamines		
Yes	23 (58)	17 (42)
No	14 (29)	35 (71)
	$X^2 = 6.44 < .05$	
Have had difficulty obtaining marihuana		
Yes	30 (52)	28 (48)
No	7 (23)	23 (77)
	$X^2 = 5.43 < .05$	

*All 2 x 2 tables are corrected by Yates correction for continuity.
Percentages are in parentheses.

Statistically significant comparisons of those who anticipate smoking in 10 years and those who do not are presented in Table 4.4. The striking feature of the collectivity of significant variables is that all are insome way related to marihuana itself.

Variables associated with the absence of the anticipation of smoking marihuana 10 years hence are: less frequent use of marihuan each week, older age on occasion of first use of marihuana, less apt to have gotten high at time of the first marihuana smoking experience, relative infrequency of having a member of family who smokes mari-huana, and the less frequent mention of enjoyment as a reason for continued use of marihuana.

Initiation to Marihuana. Those who did not try marihuana at their first opportunity to do so were assumed to have been deterred. Clearly this is using the deterrence concept in a different manner

TABLE 4.3

Characteristics Associated with Having Tried
Marihuana at First Opportunity

Characteristic	Tried at First Opportunity*	
	Yes	No
Race		
Black	23 (44)	29 (56)
White	28 (76)	9 (24)
$X^2 = 7.50 < .01$		
Desire to try		
Additional drugs		
Yes	22 (73)	8 (27)
No	28 (48)	30 (52)
$X^2 = 4.09 < .05$		
Status		
College	22 (73)	8 (27)
Prison	15 (52)	14 (48)
Chicago blacks	14 (47)	16 (53)
$X^2 = 4.91 < .10$		

*All 2 x 2 tables are corrected by Yates correction for con-tinuity. Percentages are in parentheses.

TABLE 4.4

Characteristics Associated with the Expectation
to Smoke Marihuana 10 Years Hence

Characteristic	Smoking 10 Years Hence*	
	Yes	No
Frequency of marihuana use		
Two or more times		
per week	39 (74)	14 (26)
Less than 2 times		
per week	8 (40)	12 (60)
	$X^2 = 5.75 < .05$	
Age at first use of		
marihuana		
16 or under	32 (78)	9 (22)
17 or over	15 (47)	17 (53)
	$X^2 = 6.318 < .05$	
Got high the first time smoked		
Yes	29 (78)	8 (22)
No	12 (50)	12 (50)
	$X^2 = 4.11 < .05$	
Member of family who		
smokes marihuana		
Yes	24 (77)	7 (23)
No	21 (54)	18 (46)
	$X^2 = 3.22 < .10$	
Feel there is something		
bad about the use of		
marihuana		
Yes	16 (50)	16 (50)
No	30 (75)	10 (25)
	$X^2 = 3.79 < .10$	
Enjoyment as reason		
for continued use		
Yes	36 (78)	10 (22)
No	11 (46)	13 (54)
	$X^2 = 6.12 < .05$	

*All 2 x 2 tables corrected by Yates correction for continuity.
Percentages are in parentheses.

from the use of the concept in the previous category ("fear of being caught"). However, it is consistent with the view of deterrence in the broader socializing, habituating sense (Hawkins, 1969). It may be assumed that the individual who restrained himself from the opportunity to try marihuana was "deterred" by some norm or collectivity of norms and the corresponding values.

Of the subjects, 38 did not smoke marihuana on their first opportunity to do so. This opportunity had been a multi-occasion event for all but four of our responding subjects.[3] Opportunities to smoke were rejected by 21 on 4 or more occasions before trying marihuana for the first time.

Of 36 subjects who gave reasons for not trying marihuana, 18 were afraid it might be harmful, 3 were afraid of being caught, 4 were not interested or curious, 6 said they really didn't know what it was, and 5 gave varied responses not classifiable in these categories. The haunting specter of threat and uncertainty associated with conventional views of deterrence is explicit in most of these responses.

It was anticipated that the initiation to marihuana, whether it was precipitous or entered into after a number of opportunities, would produce a number of distinguishing characteristics. As evidenced in Table 4.3, this expectation was not borne out. Only 3 variables distinguished the 2 groups.

The distinguishing pattern suggested here is different than the previously considered variable ("fear of being caught"). The present criteria suggest, for example, that whites are least apt to be deterred. Also, the prison population and ghetto blacks were more apt to have chosen not to have smoked marihuana at their first opportunity to do so. Those who do not aspire to try additional drugs were also most apt to have rejected the first opportunity to try marihuana.

Discussion

The data suggests that there are instances in which experienced marihuana smokers have been deterred. This evidence in itself is in direct contrast to the usual assertions that are made about marihuana smokers, particularly established marihuana smokers, as represented in the sample. Schaps and Sanders (1970), for example, present evidence which indicates that the naive and established marihuana smokers are the most apt to be careless in their smoking habits. This in turn suggests that the deterrent principle may not be applicable to these groups. The present data indicates, however, that for the established smokers studied, a sizable proportion (41%) had experienced a situation in which they admitted to having been deterred. This, then, is additional evidence to add to the arguments presented

at the beginning of this paper regarding the applicability of the deterrent model to marihuana. The evidence of deterrence among established marihuana smokers adds credence to the possibility of a viable
deterrent model in the control of marihuana. It would be interesting
to study persons who have had only limited marihuana smoking experience, as well as a group of persons without any marihuana experience, to see to what extent they have been in situations in which
they have exercised restraint because of the fear of being caught.

While the data indicates that there is a deterrent mechanism
which operates on some occasions even with the experienced marihuana smoker, the operation of this mechanism in a wide variety of
life situations should not be overlooked. Deterrence may function as
a latent element in many measures of socialization and social control.
One might, for example, be able to identify an operating deterrent
element in a system which was ostensibly designed for implementing
the rehabilitative ideal. In this situation, it would be a latent and
unintended consequence.

Caution should be exercised in rushing to embrace the deterrent position for the control of marihuana smoking. Just because
there is some evidence of deterrence does not mean that this model
is the ideal way to deal with marihuana smoking. Given the current
attitudes of acceptance or tolerance of marihuana smoking on the
part of many, efforts to apply the deterrent point of view may be
counterproductive. Indeed, current police efforts to enforce laws
in this area might well be placed in the counterproductive category.
In a democratic society, if deterrence is to be a viable control mechanism, it requires support and commitment founded on a broad base
in the judicial system and in supporting social values.

Notes

1. But surely the typically, casually oriented marihuana smoker
approaches this condition much more closely than the compulsively
oriented heroin addict whose demand for heroin is highly inelastic.

2. Chi square is used as a measure of significance. Comparisons
which are significant at the .10 level are presented in table form and
discussed. This level of significance was felt to be acceptable in view
of the exploratory nature of the study.

3. One subject did not say how many times he had an opportunity
to smoke marihuana before doing so.

References

Grupp, Stanley E.
1971   Prior criminal record and adult marihuana arrest disposi-
        tions. Journal of Criminal Law, Criminology and Police
        Science, 62: 974-79.

Grupp, Stanely E., and James V. Koch
1971   The economics of drug law enforcement. Paper presented
        at American Association for Advancement of Science,
        Philadelphia, December 26.

Grupp, Stanley E., and Warren C. Lucas
1970   The "marihuana muddle" as reflected in California arrest
        statistics and court dispositions. Law and Society Review,
        5: 251-69,

Hawkins, Gordon
1969   Punishment and deterrence: The educative, moralizing,
        and habituative effects. Wisconsin Law Review, 550-65;
        reprinted in Stanley E. Grupp (ed.), Theories of Punishment.
        Bloomington, Ind.: Indiana University Press, 1971.

Schaps, Eric, and Clinton R. Sanders
1970   Purposes, patterns, and protection in a campus drug using
        community. Journal of Health and Social Behavior, 11:
        135-45.

5

DETERRENCE AND
KNOWLEDGE OF SANCTIONS
Richard L. Henshel

It is my thesis that empirical investigation of sanctions and deterrence has unfortunately neglected an essential point, so central that its absence calls into question the conclusions of most work that has been done—although for some the data could be reanalyzed. The point referred to is that of public knowledge. People are deterred (if at all) by what they think is the certainty of capture, and by what they think is the severity of the sanction, not by what the certainty and severity is objectively. It is my purpose to describe this deficiency in research and to explore its theoretical basis.[1] Strangely, many theoretical discussions of deterrence have correctly discerned the problem, yet their insight has rarely, and only very recently, been translated or incorporated into empirical inquiry. Even more strangely, other empirical work in criminology has explicitly demonstrated the shaky basis of most extant deterrence research, yet the two traditions have but rarely come into contact. The fact that this has occurred not only within the same discipline but even within a single "specialty" raises interesting questions of communication which transcend criminology.

To state the problem forthrightly, most empirical research on deterrence has been done in ways which do not permit the kinds of interpretation which have been made. Even after decades of study, after position statements by an impressive array of experts (Ehrmann, 1962), there is still no valid knowledge regarding the efficacy of

I am indebted to Theodore Chiricos, David Edwards, Walter Firey, Jack Gibbs, and Gordon Waldo for their helpful suggestions. An earlier version of this paper was presented at the Eastern Sociological Society meetings, Boston, April 1972.

capital punishment, and the same is true a _fortiori_ of the deterrent
efficacy of other sanctions. Inasmuch as important policy decisions
may be based on studies of deterrence, and inasmuch as sociological
theory ultimately takes them into account, the conceptual error become
of more than marginal importance.[2]

The effects of sanctions on deviant conduct has for decades been
a central question of sociology. From time to time American social
science has manifested extreme skepticism as to the efficacy of legal
punishment upon the pervasiveness of crime, maintaining that deterren
doctrines are outmoded and totally out of place in modern society (Ball
1955; Gibbs, 1966; Toby, 1964). Punishment has been seen as a barbar
hangover from primitive beliefs in lex talionis, an eye for an eye (see
Menninger, 1968). Occasionally reference was made to the certainty
and swiftness of sanctions; rarely during this period to severity as a
deterrent factor. Later, however, and commendably, increased resistance was shown to this facile approach, and serious challenge to the
beliefs on which it was based. The theoretical hiatus which results
when, uniquely among forms of social control, the legal sanction alone
is denied all efficacy, has been noted. What was for long a polemical
issue has thus come to be identified as a legitimate topic for empirical
examination.

The history of empirical research on deterrence may be viewed
as progressing through a number of stages with increasing sophisti
cation—a process which is by no means terminated. Subsequent to the
pre-investigation era was a period of exclusive concentration on the
death penalty. Of the half-dozen empirical studies of general deterren
prior to 1960, virtually all pertained to capital punishment. These
are summarized in Sutherland and Cressey (1970: 330-6). In the 1960
and later, this trickle started to swell into a torrent of empirical
effort, principally located in journal articles and presented papers.
Writers have called attention to the dangers inherent in rejecting so
broad a doctrine purely on the lack of proven deterrent differential
between capital punishment (when actually applied) and life imprisonment, and have begun to direct their attention to other deterrent
situations, e.g., such seemingly simple matters as severity of parking
fines.[3] The phase was also marked by increasingly sophisticated
measures of severity and certainty, but not by an overwhelming increase in theoretical sophistication.

Theoretically, deterrence has a distinctive meaning which has
become increasingly significant in the research effort. The importanc
of considering the penalties actually imposed rather than the legal
possibilities has received increasing attention, beginning with Gibbs
(1968) and culminating in the careful attention to this consideration
in Jayewardene (1972). Nevertheless, there are certain anticipations,
going back to Ball (1955) among modern criminologists, and in other

ways to Bentham (1843) and Tarde (1912), on the importance of ascertaining what people think the sanctioning outcomes are.

Deterministic Man Versus the Perfectly Informed Hedonist: An Unconscious Resurrection

Deterrence studies have taken the form of comparing crime rates (dependent variable) under varying conditions of severity, certainty, and celerity of the legal sanction.[4] Such studies indeed have the advantage of accessible data and relatively high level of measurement (Cushing, 1969: 207). Their critical weakness is that they ignore the central theoretical conception that deterrence is in the mind of the beholder. Deterrence, when and if it exists, is a state of mind.[5] If the mind in question holds no cognition relative to the punitive sanction (i.e., it has not been heard of, believed in, or felt applicable), then the objective existence of sanctions with specified levels of severity, certainty, swiftness is of no consequence—deterrence in the particular instance cannot exist for this person, but not because deterrence as a general phenomenon does not exist. By concentrating on the objective properties of the legal sanction, studies have presumed that these objective properties are actually correctly conceptualized by the people, or at least by a sufficient number of them. Or, at least, that errors are randomly distributed. These assumptions, as shall be seen, may be very unlikely indeed.

Modern opponents of punishment for long adopted a deterministic, mechanistic model of man. Man did as he had been "programmed" by his genes, experiences, and/or associations. Punishment was therefore ineffective and, being of no effect, it was barbarous. In contrast, later empirical approach to deterrence has, implicitly or explicitly, put this assumption to the test. But in so doing it has only contrasted the viability of two extreme models of man: the human being as mechanism versus the completely free, rational actor. Thus a robot is pitted against "rational man," with no testing of yet a third posture: a conception of man as goal-seeking but not information-seeking. Such a man might indeed be swayed by severity of punishment, for example, but only if he "stumbled" on the news, and only if he believed it where it appeared to contradict, e.g., television drama. That this hypothetical man bears a suspicious resemblance to what much sociological literature depicts is a severe indictment of deterrence research, for investigators in deterrence have virtually ignored him.[6] If the earliest criminologists and penologists assumed a calculating, hedonistic man, and if their reformist replacements assumed a preprogrammed, noncalculating man, the new penal positivists, even while rationally contrasting the two above, have taken the perfectly informed man, or at

53

least his cousin the adequately informed man, as the only alternative to mechanism. This is not a consciously chosen position, but one implicit in their entire mode of research.[7] The specific models of man chosen for contrast in many respects delimit the possible conclusions (Kunkel and Garrick, 1969).

It is certainly possible that the difference in severity between execution and life imprisonment really does not deter people from crimes which may legally result in capital punishment. (Homicide in particular is among the crimes least subject to influence by any known means.) What is essential is that this is not presently known, and indeed is not knowable, simply by comparing capital crime rates acros jurisdictions that do or do not have capital punishment, for it may be that potential offenders do not know the law for capital-type crimes in their jurisdiction, but would act in accordance with severity if they knew it. Nor is it to be ascertained by comparisons across time, in which either executions have occurred or laws changed, unless it can be shown that the public was aware of such changes. The extent of public awareness of sanctioning outcomes has been neglected in studies of the efficacy of capital punishment. What if, as seems intuitively likely, the residents of two adjoining jurisdictions, only one of which provided capital punishment, were not aware of the true state of their laws? What if the survey were to reveal that public belief about the existence of the death penalty in a given jurisdiction was virtually independent of whether or not it actually existed therein?[8] Substantial independence of objective reality and public belief, while definitely not an affirmation of deterrent efficacy, would necessitate a complete reanalysis (where possible) of studies which have failed to consider their implicit assumption of public awareness, and would in addition require new research based on the correct problem of whether the people's assumptions about the existence and application of a particula penalty may deter them from the crime it is prescribed for.

The Importance of Public Knowledge

Examining criminal sanctions in general, it must be asked whether in point of fact the public knows the sanctions applicable under the law. To what extent is the objective likelihood of receiving a sentence of given severity for a given act correctly perceived? What of perceptions of the probable certainty and swiftness of these sanctions, or of perceptions of "effective" sentence length—e.g., after parole is included? Evidence from a separate research tradition indicates that the public is in fact terribly ignorant, and typically in error, on such matters. Nor are the large errors necessarily random in nature. It is important—vital, in fact—that public ignorance be more

54

than a mere hypothesis, however plausible. For as data emerges which shows such ignorance, the burden of proof shifts and it now becomes incumbent upon those deterrence researchers utilizing one of the traditional approaches to demonstrate that, in spite of widespread ignorance, there remain substantial residual differences in perception between different times or jurisdictions. Otherwise, a failure to detect a deterrent effect ceases to illustrate inefficacy of the given sanctioning differential itself and becomes merely the outcome to be expected where public anticipations are not systematically different.

Perhaps the most important study of public knowledge has been conducted in California by the Assembly Committee on Criminal Procedure (1968), which is quite convincing in its demonstration of the public's ignorance—both of existing severity and of recent changes in severity:

> A range of 21% to 49% of the respondents had complete ignorance or were unable to even guess the maximum sentences for these crimes. Furthermore, even among those who made an estimate, the percent of correct responses ranged from 8 to 39%. If one combined the number of correct responses into a single index score of accuracy, no one person correctly answered all 11 questions about penalties, while, at the other extreme, 69% of the respondents answered 3 or less items correctly (Italics deleted).

It is significant that perceptual errors were not "unbiased"; a general tendency to underestimate penalties became clear. In the study's own words, the Californians surveyed "were extremely ignorant about penalties for crimes . . . the general public simply does not know what the penalties are." Interestingly, while the investigation uncovers ample evidence to require gross reanalysis for most existing deterrence studies, the investigators believe instead that they have demonstrated the general inefficacy of punishment because only convicts apparently know anything at all about the magnitude of the sanctions. But of course they would have demonstrated this only if the surveyed individuals were incapable of learning any more than they knew, which no one wishes to claim. For that matter, many Californians may be deterred by their misconceptions of the law—in Thomas' celebrated phrase, situations defined as real are real in their consequences.

Not only was the California sample ignorant of the nature of recent changes in criminal law, but the people were on the whole unaware that alterations of any sort had been made. Similarly, Walker and Argyle (1964) found some 76% of an English sample were unaware that the law against attempted suicide had been abolished. A poll in

Nebraska, reported in Zimring and Hawkins (1973: 143), found 41% of adult males thought that the state's long-standing bad-check law would not apply if restitution was made.[9] Similar findings of public ignorance with respect to certainty of apprehension are briefly reported in Jensen (1969: 200).

Numerous traditions within sociology have explored factors which would predict public ignorance of these matters. Requirements of space prohibit extended treatment, but sociologists have devoted considerable attention to difficulties in getting correct information— bureaucratic secretiveness, complexity of legal machinery, inadequacies of criminal statistics, protection of information (e.g., in juvenile court), the free press-fair trial clash, and selective coverage by the press.[10] The distribution of knowledge in society is often viewed as structured in terms of individual relevances (Berger and Luckmann, 1966: 45). Sanctioning outcomes are not typically part of the pragmatically necessary knowledge of men in modern society, with the possible exception of professional criminals and criminal lawyers. Equally important is the ease of obtaining erroneous information via fictional drama. Thus the hours spent by the average television viewer before the screen, as well as the frequency (and breakdown) of various incidents of violence, have been counted on numerous occasions. It is well known that the network system of television produces reliance on "formula plots," of which the murder trial with lurking death penalty has been a stock-in-trade. It is no wonder that public ignorance of sanctioning outcomes is all but ubiquitous under such constraints. What might be a source of wonder is that the above analytical traditions could exist alongside efforts in deterrence research with so little stimulation to the latter.[11]

At this point, one must examine precisely why objective sanctioning differences without variations in rates of deviance do not preclude the possibility that the sanctioning differential might reduce the proscribed behavior. A complete answer to this question would require a general theory of punishment, but one might begin by demonstrating the central position of public knowledge in the relation between sanctions and deviance. Figure 5.1 depicts the alternative explanations for a negative relation between formal sanctions and deviance. (It should be distinguished from an overall analysis of the inhibitors of deviance; see Blake and Davis, 1964: 477-481, for an attempt at this task.) The two traditional explanations are deterrence and consensual reaffirmation of the norm. Deterrence, stated very crudely, assumes that cases of punishment produce fear of the consequences in would-be offenders, leading to a decline in deviance. The essentially Durkheimian notion of strengthened consensus assumes that cases of punishment primarily serve as reaffirmation of the community norms, but extensions propose that this thereby mobilizes the informal social

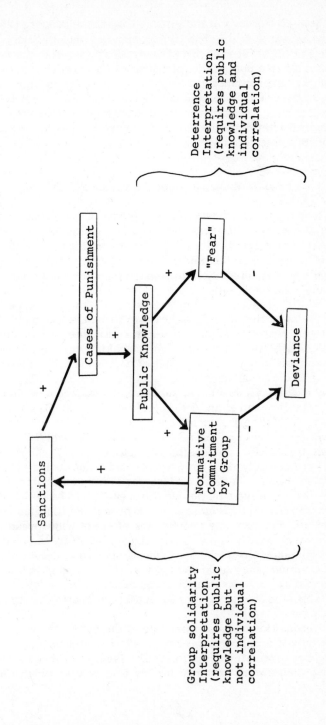

FIGURE 5.1

Relations of Sanctions and Deviance

Deterrence
Interpretation
(requires public
knowledge and
individual
correlation)

Cases of Punishment

"Fear"

Public Knowledge

Deviance

Sanctions

Normative
Commitment
by Group

Group solidarity
Interpretation
(requires public
knowledge but
not individual
correlation)

disapproval which may itself diminish deviance (Coser, 1967; see also Erikson, 1966: 3-4.)[12] The two conceptions thus provide alternative (nonconflicting) bases for the efficacy of punishment as a reducer of crime. Both are potential explanations of a negative relation between sanctioning and deviance, and are the only positions which do so.[13] This is significant since both positions tacitly require public knowledge. Public knowledge (or ignorance) thus emerges as the great virtually unexamined intervening variable, irrespective of which candidate interpretation is considered.[14]

Public Knowledge and Deterrence Research

It is clear that most existing studies of deterrence have unconsciously related differences in objective sanctions to corresponding objective crime rates, without sufficient examination of the deterrence concept to recognize the hidden intermediary. Of course, if the only objective of a given study is to find out whether, in the particular instances examined, objective sanctioning differences correspond to objective differences in the crime rate, this can indeed be ascertained. Examination of the discourse, however, reveals that most if not all deterrence research is undertaken to contribute more than a mere historical account of a specific relationship: researchers intend that their analysis should become part of a growing set of generalizations relating to the broad questions of deterrence. There is no need to display exegetical skill here; such statements are ubiquitous in the deterrence literature, and I shall refrain from singling out individual authors. Tentative judgments have been passed on the efficacy of general deterrence, on the relative potency of severity and certainty, on their interaction, on possible boundaries and thresholds.[15]

Unfortunately, it is only where public knowledge is reasonably accurate (and errors more or less randomly distributed) that the efficacy of objective sanctioning differences can be correctly appraised by the standard, traditional research procedure (Chiricos and Waldo, 1970: 215). The possibly confounding effect of widespread ignorance is still not generally appreciated, and public awareness has not therefore been ascertained in most existing studies of deterrence.[16] In view of the fact that separate and distinct studies of public awareness of sanctioning outcomes find it to be discouragingly low, the validity of the reported findings with respect to deterrent efficacy is open to serious challenge.

Recognition of the importance of the public awareness dimension slowly moved forward in the early 1970s, over a decade after the emergence of empirical studies. The factor is acknowledged but not explored in the work of the Assembly Committee (1968), Chiricos and

Waldo (1970: 215), Morris and Zimring (1969: 145), Van den Haag (1969: 146), and Wilkins (1969: 17-18, 160-161). Hints are found in Tittle (1969b: 422), Crowther (1969: 153), and Gibbs (1968: 530). With the exception of Ball's classic paper (1955), there was virtually no recognition within modern criminology until Zimring and Hawkins (1973) treated the matter theoretically, and Waldo and Chiricos (1972) treated it empirically.

But none of these creative efforts is as "tough" on earlier research as seems to be necessary. In a spirit of cohesiveness, some even pay homage to the conclusions of their predecessors. Homage to the empirical emphasis which these pioneers displayed is well deserved, but acquiescence to their conclusions is inappropriate. Logic would seem to require the position that most earlier deterrence research must either be reanalyzed (where this is still possible), interpreted far more narrowly that its originators intended, or, reluctantly, in some cases disregarded. The analysts' implicit models of man have been too long and too seriously ignored.

Notes

1. It is instructive that many of the earlier "unfinished problems" in the study of deterrence (e.g., Cushing, 1969; Morris and Zimring, 1969; Tittle, 1969a) neglected this central issue of knowledge and perception. More recent lists have begun to include it.

2. As an example of the policy component, one of the central tasks of the Law Reform Commission of Canada (a permanent official body) is to evaluate the effects of laws, including the deterrent and rehabilitative consequences of the criminal law.

3. See, e.g., Chambliss (1966) and Beutel (1957). The possibility of "thresholds" has also been raised. It may be observed that the denial of general deterrent efficacy also runs counter to the concept of vicarious reinforcement in theories of learning. The criticisms of earlier arguments and studies are summarized succinctly in Gibbs (1968) and Tittle (1969b).

4. For a survey of alternative measures of these factors, see Kuykendall (1969: Ch. II).

5. This is not to say that sanctions necessarily have no effects other than deterrence. Venerable theories have related the application of formal sanctions to the strength of the normative order (what is sometimes called their "general prevention" function). In this paper, I am exclusively concerned with general deterrence—the influence of sanctions on members of society at large—and not with special deterrence—the influence on individuals actually punished. For excellent treatment of these and other important distinctions, see Morris and Zimring (1969).

6. As Gibbs notes (1968: 518, 530), as yet there is no updated restatement of the theory of deterrence, although this situation may at last be changing (see Zimring and Hawkins, 1973). Classical doctrines are stated in terms of ideas such as "free will" and indeterminism" which are grossly out of place in contemporary social science. Given this hiatus, it is no wonder that modern researchers have taken the classical doctrine at face value and thus contrasted only two extreme conceptions of man. Yet deterrence can also be formulated in terms of modern reinforcement theory—a position "uncontaminated" by association with indeterminism.

7. Nelson (1966: 317) points out that a similar problem confronts the traditional economist. He suggests replacing rational economic man with rational but ill-informed man. Every man has truly the best information about his own utilities, but experts have far better information about the usual consequences of acts. "The assumption that an individual always has the maximum information relevant to decisions about his consumption is an exceedingly strong assumption. It is no wonder that non-economists almost universally reject it."

8. This is not implausible. If the average adult watches hours of television drama each week, if television programs deal with death beyond the point of monotony, and if they invariably associate murder (the typical crime displayed) with the death penalty, how well, indeed, does the citizen know the laws of his locale? As Van den Haag (1969: 146) puts it: "Contrary to what Professor Sellin et al. seem to presume, I doubt that offenders are aware of the absence or presence of the death penalty state by state or period by period." It would be instructive (if no longer possible) to determine whether a single jurisdiction existed in the United States at the time of Sellin's studies in which the majority of adults did not believe that the death penalty existed in their locale. As shall be seen, knowledge about sanctions is indeed low.

9. The proportion of public error may be exaggerated somewhat because of low enforcement level.

10. On this last factor, it is interesting that at the time of the survey of McCafferty (1954: 36-41), four states prohibited publication of any official statement on an execution with details other than that a prisoner had been executed according to law.

11. It is interesting that classical legal philosophers were frequently cognizant of the importance of public knowledge.

12. Since knowledge of deviations may tend per se to lower normative consensus, it is arguable whether punishment actually heightens normative consensus beyond previous levels or merely restores it to the status quo ante. In spite of the age of Durkheim's interpretation there have been few efforts at verification. Exploratory efforts are presented in Jensen (1969), Walker and Argyle (1964), and Salem and Bowers (1969).

13. The doctrine of disablement or incapacitation, although typically punishing in consequences, actually reflects a mistrust of the efficacy of deterrence as a means to reduce crime.

14. This paper emphasizes deterrence, but most of the comments concerning public knowledge apply as well to collective reaffirmation. Though similar in their dependence upon public knowledge, the two differ in their amenability to ecological correlation. Whereas the same individual must be knowledgeable and restrained under a deterrence conception, the solidarity approach could accept knowledge and constraint in different persons. See a discussion of similar issues in Waldo and Chiricos (1972).

15. Some readers have felt that these researchers were really not unaware of this failing of their research, but simply determined to get on with the job with the tools at hand. The literature has been specifically scrutinized for signs of such recognition, but it is simply not encountered in the empirical work on deterrence until circa 1970 or 1971, even among writers who scrupulously enumerated the other shortcomings of their research. Even those earlier workers who used a perceptual approach did not analyze the inherent drawbacks of the "objective" method. Historically, the writer, presenting a guest seminar on these drawbacks at Florida State University in the spring of 1971, was surprised to find that Theodore Chiricos and Gordon Waldo were independently developing the same idea.

16. Alternative means of resolving this problem were suggested in an earlier version of this paper. In essence there are two intertwined difficulties with public knowledge as a variable. The first and simpler problem is the possibility of disparity between knowledge about the penalty in general and perceptions about how it would be applied to the individual himself. Use of multiple questions to tap both dimensions has been employed here. The second difficulty involves Robinson's "ecological fallacy" (1950), which may distort findings based on surveys of public knowledge and victimization. Significantly, it could also bias traditional studies of deterrence as well. The "ecological fallacy" would be relevant under the "fear of consequences" interpretation, but not under Durkheim's "reaffirmation of the norm" interpretation (see Figure 5.1). One way out is to abandon public knowledge in favor of individual perception, and relate each person's concept of the sanctions with his self-admitted violations (Waldo and Chiricos, 1972). However while this approach is defensible for minor crimes, it does not seem feasible for the study of very serious offenses.

References

Assembly Committee on Criminal Procedure (State of California)
  1968 Part one—Survey of knowledge of criminal penalties. De-
        terrent Effects of Criminal Sanctions (Progress Report,
        May): 9-20.

Ball, John C.
  1955 The deterrence concept in criminology and law. Journal of
        Criminal Law, Criminology, and Police Science, 46: 347-54.

Bentham, Jeremy
  1843 Principles of penal law. Works, Volume 1, Edinburgh: Tait.

Berger, Peter L., and Thomas Luckmann
  1966 The Social Construction of Reality. Garden City: Doubleday

Beutel, Frederick K.
  1957 Some Potentialities of Experimental Jurisprudence as a
        New Branch of Social Science. Lincoln: University of
        Nebraska Press.

Blake, Judith, and Kingsley Davis
  1964 Norms, values, and sanctions. In Robert E. L. Faris (ed.),
        Handbook of Modern Sociology. Chicago: Rand McNally.

Chambliss, William J.
  1966 The deterrent influence of punishment. Crime and Delin-
        quency, 12(January): 70-75.

Chiricos, Theodore G., and Gordon P. Waldo
  1970 Punishment and crime: An examination of some empirical
        evidence. Social Problems, 18: 200-17.

Coser, Lewis A.
  1967 Continuities in the Study of Social Conflict. New York:
        Free Press.

Crowther, Carol
  1969 Crime, penalties, and legislatures. Annals of the American
        Academy of Political and Social Science, 381: 147-58.

Cushing, Robert G.
  1969 The relative impact of changing urban characteristics,
        adequacy of law enforcement resources, and punishment

on the incidence and nature of major crime. Proceedings, Annual Convention, Southwestern Sociological Association.

Ehrmann, Sara R.
1962   For whom the chair waits. Federal Probation, 26 (March): 14-25.

Erikson, Kai T.
1966   Wayward Puritans. New York: Wiley.

Gibbs, Jack P.
1966   Sanctions. Social Problems 14: 147-59.
1968   Crime, punishment and deterrence.
Southwestern Social Science Quarterly, 48:515-30.

Jayewardene, C. H. S.
1972   Homicide and punishment: A study in deterrence. Paper presented to the Canadian Sociology and Anthropology Association.

Jensen, Gary F.
1969   "Crime doesn't pay": Correlates of a shared misunderstanding. Social Problems, 17: 189-201.

Kunkel, John H., and Michael A. Garrick
1969   Models of man in sociological analysis. Social Science Quarterly, 50 (June): 136-52.

Kuykendall, Helen K.
1969   The Deterrent Efficacy of Punishment. Masters thesis, University of Texas.

McCafferty, James A.
1954   Capital Punishment in the United States: 1930 to 1952. Masters thesis, Ohio State University.

Menninger, Karl
1968   The Crime of Punishment. New York: Viking Press.

Morris, Norval, and Frank Zimring
1969   Deterrence and corrections. Annals of the American Academy of Political and Social Science 381: 137-46.

Nelson, Philip J.
1966   An essay in normative economics. Social Research, 33: 314-31.

Robinson, W. S.
   1950   Ecological correlations and the behavior of individuals.
          American Sociological Review, 15: 351-57.

Salem, Richard G., and William J. Bowers
   1969   The deterrent effects of formal sanctions. Paper presented
          to American Sociological Association.

Sutherland, Edwin H., and Donald R. Cressey
   1970   Criminology. Philadelphia: Lippincott.

Tarde, Gabriel
   1912   Penal Philosophy. Boston: Little, Brown.

Tittle, Charles R.
   1969a   Crime and deterrence. Paper presented to American
           Sociological Association.

   1969b   Crime rates and legal sanctions. Social Problems, 16:
           409-23.

Toby, Jackson
   1964   Is punishment necessary? Journal of Criminal Law, Crimi-
          nology, and Police Science, 55: 332-33.

Van den Haag, Ernest
   1969   On deterrence and the death penalty. Journal of Criminal
          Law, Criminology, and Police Science 60: 141-47.

Waldo, Gordon P., and Theodore Chiricos
   1972   Perceived penal sanction and self-reported criminality: A
          neglected approach to deterrence research. Social Problems
          20: 522-40.

Walker, Nigel, and Michael Argyle
   1964   Does the law affect moral judgments? British Journal of
          Criminology, 4(October): 570-81.

Wilkins, Leslie T.
   1969   Evaluation of Penal Measures. New York: Random.

Zimring, Franklin, and Gordon Hawkins
   1973   Deterrence. Chicago: University of Chicago Press.

6

POLICE BACKGROUND
CHARACTERISTICS AND
PERFORMANCE: FINDINGS
Bernard Cohen

For this study, information was obtained about the background and performance of 1,915 officers appointed to the New York City Police Department in 1957, of whom 1,608 were still active members of the force in 1968 when most of the data were collected.[1] The objectives of the study were:

1. To develop information on how to select men who are likely to perform effectively as police officers and to reject candidates likely to be unsatisfactory.

2. To identify attributes currently thought to be negative or positive indicators which in fact are not related to later good or poor performance.

3. To identify methods for sharpening the estimate of a recruit's future performance by using information from his probationary period on the force, and for determining which probationary patrolmen should be terminated.

4. To determine the kind of men who are likely to perform ineffectively in areas where complaints against the police are common.

In the present study, only quantifiable measures of background and performance, of a type commonly maintained in personnel files by police departments, were utilized. No personality tests were administered to the subjects, nor were any special performance evaluations undertaken. The study differs from those previously completed in the following ways:

1. All the subjects were officers in a single Police Department, and yet the sample size is large enough to study interesting subgroups such as black officers, detectives, and college-educated men. Regrettably, there were not enough Puerto Rican officers in the sample to analyze their performance separately from that of other officers.

2. All the subjects entered the Police Department in a single year. The use of such a cohort design automatically standardizes for the tenure of the subjects and assures that they all experienced a similar sequence of departmental policies in regard to assignment and promotion.

3. Nearly every officer who entered the Department in the selected year is included as a subject. There was no need to request men to volunteer to cooperate with the study, and thus such biases as may be introduced through the use of volunteers were not present.

4. The study was not confined to officers of a particular rank. In fact, the entire range from patrolman to captain is represented in the sample. Thus, it is possible to use career advancement as a measure of performance.

5. All of the data was collected at least 11 years after the subject's appointment, thus providing a substantial period of time over which to measure performance. This also permits analysis of the relationship of early job performance and experience to later job performance.

6. Although most of the performance measures rely on the documented actions taken by the Department in respect to each officer, and thus reflect the policeman's view of performance, there is also extensive data on two community-derived (albeit negative) measures of performance. These are the number of civilian complaints against officers (i.e., complaints of the use of unnecessary force, abuse of authority, discourteous behavior, and ethnic slurs) and the number of allegations of harassment (i.e., false arrest, illegal search and seizure, detention of a person without cause, etc.).

Methodology

Most of the data for this study was collected manually from the files of several units within the New York City Police Department, including the Chief Clerk's Personnel Unit, the Disciplinary Record Unit, the Medical Unit, the Office of the Chief of Detectives, the Civilian Complaint Review Board, and the Background Investigation and Screening Unit. A total of 150 descriptors were gathered for each subject.

Some of these factors describe the subject's personal background and early performance on the force, such as his race, age, I.Q., civil service score, occupational history, military history, incidents involving police and courts, and probationary evaluation. Other factors relate to the officer's performance on the job, including career advancement, awards, internal disciplinary actions, civilian complaints, and medical history.

Data Analysis. The relations between predictor variables and individual performance measures, as well as the relations among the performance measures taken as a group, were first determined from cross-tabulations and simple correlations.[2] These tabulations were obtained separately for the black officers and the total active cohort, which predominately consists of white officers. Next, the variables from the cross-tabulations which appeared to be interesting for further study were processed by factor analysis.

Finally, the strength of each background variable as a predictor of later performance was determined by step-wise multiple linear regression.

Relationships Between Early Background
Characteristics and Performance

The following discussion summarizes briefly the relationships found between the predictor variables (early background character-istics) and other characteristics of background and performance.

Race. The first background descriptor is the race of the officer. It was possible to compare the characteristics of black officers with those of white officers, but the number of Hispanic officers was too small to permit statistical analysis of their differences from the others.

Some of the important differences in the background character-istics of white and black officers appointed in 1957 were as follows:

1. The black officers were slightly older than the whites at time of appointment, and more of them were married.

2. More black officers than white officers were born outside New York City: 29% of the blacks compared to 6% of the whites.

3. The fathers of white applicants ranked higher than the fathers of black applicants on the scale of prestige used in this study, but the prestige rankings of the occupations of the candidates themselves did not differ by race.

4. The black officers were considerably better educated than the whites. In fact, nearly 40% of the black appointees had attended college for at least one year, compared to somewhat over 20% of the whites.

There were some interesting characteristics on which black and white officers did not differ. No differences by race were found on I.Q. or civil service scores, which means that for each range of scores the fractions of black appointees in that range was about the same as their fraction of the total group. It should be noted, however, that every officer in the sample had passed the civil service examination for patrolman, and therefore there is no information about the proportions by race among the men who took the examination but failed. Finally, black officers and white officers did not differ on any aspect of military or employment history, arrest or summons history, or in the number of times they appeared in civil court.

Despite these important factors on which the blacks did not differ from the whites, the black appointees ranked somewhat lower on the rating by the Department's background investigator. In fact, over 25% of the blacks were rated disapproval, poor, or questionable by the background investigators, compared to 15% of the others.

There were also some important differences by race in performance after appointment. The black officers accumulated 65% more departmental disciplinary charges than white officers, but they did not differ from whites on the numbers of civilian complaints, allegations of harassment, or criminal charges.

The black officers also did not progress through civil service ranks as well as white officers. In fact, at the end of 14 years there were 5 black sergeants and 1 black lieutenant in the group, or 6% of the total, compared to 15% of the whites. However, the black officers did progress into and through the Detective Division better than whites. Almost 30% of the black officers were detectives after 14 years, compared to 15% of the white officers. These two facts about the career advancement of black officers tend to compensate for each other, so that if the two groups are compared according to their current salary, black officers have just about the same salaries as white officers, or perhaps slightly higher. The fraction of black officers who left the Department prior to 1968 was the same as the fraction of whites who terminated.

Age. The men who were oldest at time of appointment were least likely to advance beyond patrol assignment, had low absenteeism for sickness, and were substantially less likely than average to have civilian complaints. This observation does not arise from a departmental policy of placing the older officers in the least hazardous precincts; in fact, a subject's age at appointment was not found to be correlated with the hazard status of the first precinct to which he was assigned. Therefore, the data suggests that older recruits would be best suited for assignment to sensitive communities.

I.Q. In general, men with a high I.Q. advanced through the civil service route to a greater extent than men with a lower I.Q., and they had more departmental awards, but they did not differ from average on the patterns of misconduct. Men with below average I.Q. were much more likely than average to be assigned to traffic duties, at which they appeared to perform well. Black officers with high I.Q. had a greater incidence of the departmental misconduct pattern than average, including high absenteeism, but they did not have above-average career advancement. This finding is merely indicative of possible problems with relations among the races in the Department, which should be explored further by an interview study which includes some black officers with high I.Q.

Civil Service Score. The white officers who scored high on the civil service examination for appointment as a patrolman were found to be more likely than those who scored low to attain later civil service promotions to sergeant, lieutenant, or captain, but the same was not true for black officers. The civil service score was not related to any other pattern of performance, including departmental disciplinary actions, civilian complaints, or absenteeism. For white officers, a high civil service score was slightly predictive of good grades in the police academy—which was not considered to be a performance measure—but not for blacks.

In short, the civil service examination for patrolmen does not appear to predict any aspect of job performance measured in this study, other than the ability to pass later civil service examinations for promotion.

Region of Birth. Black officers born outside New York City had better career advancement, especially to detective assignments, than city-born blacks. Few of the white officers were born outside the city, and therefore no significant patterns emerged for them.

Siblings. Among black officers, those with few siblings had a history of more misconduct than those with several siblings. No such patterns were observed for white officers.

Occupational History. Occupational mobility was not found to be associated with any aspect of performance among those officers who remained on the force. However, a prior history of employment disciplinary incidents or dismissals was found to be a strong predictor of a future pattern as a disciplinary problem for the Department.

Military History. Veterans were not found to be better or worse performers than nonveterans, and the same was true for men with military commendations. However, a military disciplinary record, like an employment disciplinary record, was a predictor of future misconduct; in this case the misconduct included not only violation of the Department's rules and procedures, but also civilian complaints of unnecessary force and harassment.

Arrest History. Men who had been arrested for nonviolent crimes prior to joining the force were less likely than other officers to be later charged with harassment of citizens, such as false arrest, illegal search and seizure, etc. Seemingly, their own personal experiences tempered their relations with crime suspects. In other respects, men who had a previous history of arrest for nonviolent crimes performed no differently from other officers. Although the number of subjects with a prior arrest for a violent crime was too small to obtain statistically significant findings, the data suggested that such men had excessive misconduct later.

71

Civil Court Appearances. Men who had appeared several times in civil court as a party or witness in litigation proved more likely than average to engage in harassment later, although the differences were not large. There is some indication that a history of court appearances may reflect difficulty in getting along with other people.

Other Early Background Characteristics. Aspects of background which might be thought to be negative but which were not found to be related to later performance, among those who were appointed to the force in spite of these characteristics, included: a large number of debts, a prior history of a psychological disorder, and any history of mental disorder in the applicant's family. Other aspects of background found unrelated to performance were: father's occupation, number of residences or place of residence, marital status and number of children, and number of summonses.

Background Investigator's Rating. The Police Department's background investigators, who had access to the pre-1957 data used in this study and in addition interviewed the applicant and his neighbors and employers, were fairly successful judges of how a man would later perform as a policeman. Low-rated candidates were less likely to be promoted than high-rated candidates, and they were more frequently departmental discipline problems. In fact, 25% of those rated excellent by the background investigators were later promoted to sergeant, lieutenant, or captain, compared to 9% of those rated poor; and 42% of those rated poor later had at least one substantiated disciplinary action, compared to 16% of those rated excellent. The background investigator's rating did not distinguish men who would later have excessive civilian complaints or allegations of harassment.

Relationships Between Later Background
Characteristics and Performance

None of the early background characteristics were as strong predictors of later performance as the following variables.

Recruit Training Score. An officer's recruit training score was the strongest predictor of his later performance. Men who scored high on written examinations on the material presented in police academy training courses were subsequently much better performers than average. They advanced more rapidly through special assignments and civil service promotions, they had less departmental misconduct and absenteeism, and they had more awards than lower-scoring officers.

Among black officers, recruit score was related statistically only to later career advancement. For example, the data shows that 45% of the blacks with recruit scores of 75 and higher advanced to the

Detective Division, compared to 10% of the officers with scores below 75. Not a single black officer with recruit training score of less than 75 advanced through civil service promotion.

The overall incidence of misconduct for black officers, although not significantly related to recruit score, appeared to be consistent with the patterns observed for the white officers.

Probationary Evaluation. The officer's rating while on probation was found to be the second strongest predictor of later performance. Men who were marked "unsatisfactory" on some aspect of performance after 9 months on the force tended to have more allegations of misconduct subsequently, of which more were brought to trial and substantiated, than subjects without derogatory ratings. The statistics show, for example, that 67% of the subjects with poor rating had been alleged to have engaged in misconduct, compared to 55% of the subjects without negative ratings. Moreover, 35% of the subjects with poor probationary rating had at least one substantiated complaint on their records, while the corresponding proportion for officers without poor evaluations was 24%. These patterns reflected higher rates of violating the Department's internal rules and procedures among men with unsatisfactory probaton; these men did not have higher rates of civilian complaints, complaints characterizable as corruption, or complaints of harassment.

Subjects with poor probationary evaluations also tended to be absent more frequently than average. We found, for example, that 43% of the subjects with poor probationary ratings reported sick 11 or more times in 11 years, compared to 36% of the subjects without negative ratings.

For the black officers, the relationship between probationary evaluation and police performance was almost identical to that of the white officers. An unsatisfactory probationary rating was found to be a good predictor of above-average incidence of later departmental misconduct and absenteeism, but it was not related to other performance measures.

Education. As a group, the men with at least one year of college education who remained on the force were found to be very good performers. They advanced through civil service promotion, but not disproportionately through the detective route of advancement, and they had fewer civilian complaints than average. The men who obtained college degrees, either before or after appointment to the force, exhibited even better on-the-job performance. They advanced through preferential assignments and civil service promotions, they had low incidence of all types of misconduct except harassment, on which they were average, they had low sick time, and none of them had their firearms removed for cause.

A typical example of the difference in patterns between the college graduate and others was in the number of civilian complaints incurred over an 11-year period. The data revealed that 369 men, or 24% of the nongraduates, had a civilian complaint, compared to only 4 college graduates, or 8%. Generally speaking, the older, more educated officer received fewer civilian complaints than the younger, less educated officer.

Predicting Performance

Through multiple regression analysis, it is possible to estimate the average performance levels for officers having specified combinations of background characteristics, and to identify the background characteristics which make the greatest contribution to explaining variations in performance among officers.

The statistics show that for white officers, the strongest predictor was the recruit training score of the officer, followed by his probationary evaluation, and then his background rating. Other important background factors in approximate order of their strength of relationship were military discipline, employment discipline, education, court appearances, and age. Other background characteristics were not found to be significant predictors of later performance patterns in the regression analysis for white officers. Similarly, only three background characteristics were significantly related to later performance in the regression analysis for black officers. They were recruit training score, probationary evaluation, and court appearances.

The main observation which can be made from the data is that the two most important predictor variables were the same for both white and black officers, namely recruit training score and probationary evaluation. Information about an officer's rating on these variables is not available until several months after he has been appointed to the police force, which suggests that the selection process should not be considered to be complete until the end of the probationary period.

Conclusions

A major conclusion of this study is that it is possible to anticipate certain important aspects of job performance for black and white police officers from quantifiable information commonly maintained in personnel files by police departments. From the same data it was possible to identify some background factors which are commonly thought to be important indicators and which in fact are not related to effective or ineffective police work. The recruit training score and probationary rating, which are measures of early job performance, were found to be useful indicators of later job performance. Some background data, such as age and education, was also found to be useful in determining which men are most likely to perform ineffectively in sensitive areas of the city.

The following background characteristics were not found to be related in important ways to the performance measures, for those who were accepted by the Department and remained on the force, even if statistically significant differences were found: civil service examination score, I.Q., arrest for a petty crime, military service, military commendations, father's occupation, number of residences, aspects of early family responsibility (including marital status, number of children, and debts), reported history of psychological disorder, place of residence, and number of summonses. The hazard status of the precinct to which an officer was first assigned was reflected in the number of civilian complaints he accumulated later, but not in career advancement or other measures of performance.

The data showed that the strongest predictors of later performance are derivable from quantitative measures reflecting the subject's primary behavior and experience, as observed over a period of time. These include employment and military disciplinary actions, repeated appearances in civil court, education, and performance in the recruit academy and during the probationary period. The Police Department's background investigators are successful at weighing the information available to them at the time of application and arriving at an overall rating having predictive validity. Measures which are derived from single incidents or written examinations, such as arrest for a petty crime or low I.Q. score, are not indicative of major patterns of bad performance. In fact, arrest for a minor crime was found to be related to a low incidence of harassment after appointment.

The performance measures which proved most associated with background characteristics, in order of the amount of variance explained by the data, were career advancement, departmental misconduct, absenteeism, awards, civilian complaints, and harassment. The number of allegations of criminal misconduct, removal of firearms for cause, and invalid claims of injury were not related to the measures of background charactetistics. It seems likely that psychological tests of a type not used in this study might be needed to predict these aspects of performance.

The background factors used in this study were unable to distinguish levels of performance within the subgroup consisting of detectives. One plausible explanation for the absence of predictive validity for performance of detectives is that promotion of detectives within the Detective Division depends less on standards of performance than on other factors, such as seniority or happenstance of who may be in position to influence appointments at any given time. The finding that individual performance measures were amenable to prediction for the total active cohort, and also for certain subgroups (e.g., black officers) which were even smaller in size than the subgroup of detectives, supports the notion that both background factors and recruitment factors descriminate among subjects when actual performance differs.

Notes

1. The larger study was written by Bernard Cohen and Jan M. Chaiken. The research was conducted by the New York City-Rand Institute under a grant from the National Institute of Law Enforcement and Criminal Justice (Grant No. NI-71-030-G). The complete research findings and a detailed summary are available in two reports published by the New York City-Rand Institute.

2. Several criteria were used for assessing the importance and reliability of the relationships found by cross-tabulations, factor analysis, and regression analysis. These include: the internal consistency of associations across subclasses of the data; the degree of strength of associations; the conformability of the associations with knowledge of experienced people in the field; and formal statistical tests such as chi-square and F-tests. The statistical tests identified whether the findings differed significantly from what would be expected by chance alone. In all cases, a .05 level of significance was used, which means that there are 5 chances in 100 that two variables found to be related are actually independent of each other. All findings reported in the next section were found to be statistically significant in this sense, unless we specifically state otherwise.

**DIAL-A-COP:
A STUDY OF POLICE
MOBILIZATION**
Clifford D. Shearing

In his book, The Police and the Public, Reiss (1971) once again reiterated that policing in North America is essentially reactive in character (for an earlier statement of this position see Reiss and Bordua, 1967). To say that policing is reactive in character is to assert that police departments are organized to respond to citizen requests for service rather than to initiate police intervention. While there are no doubt a variety of reasons for this, an important one is the institutions of privacy, so fundamental to North American society and to Western society in general (Stinchcombe, 1963). These legal institutions restrict police access to private places, thereby forcing the police to rely on people who have access to such places, namely other citizens, to inform them of events that occur there. Furthermore, on most occasions, in order to enter a private place the police require an invitation from citizens.

The institutions of privacy, however, do not constitute sufficient grounds for the reactive character of North American policing, for even in the case of public places to which the police do have free access, they rely heavily on the public to inform them of trouble.[1] There appear to be at least two reasons for this:

1. Trouble is not something which is objectively defined but is rather any event that is seen to require police attention. Trouble is defined when someone "blows the whistle" (Becker, 1963). In short, trouble requires a complainant: someone who announces the presence of trouble (Emerson and Messinger, 1972).

2. Although police officers in public places can act as complainants, the probability of them being present for an event in a public place which they would define as police trouble—that is, trouble for which they feel the police are the appropriate troubleshooters[2]—is very small.

Apart from the reactive nature of police organization, the police organization for dealing with citizen complaints (that is, a citizen request that the police do somthing about some trouble) is generally highly centralized. Typically, in North America police departments, citizen requests for police intervention are processed by one central department which receives complaints and dispatches one or more police officers to the scene of the trouble. This centralization is possible because of the communications systems (two-way radios, the telephone system) and the transportation systems (the automobile, city streets, highways) available to the police and citizens in North America.

Given this organization of police departments, police officers who process citizen-initiated complaints are in a potentially powerful position for it is these officers who decide whether or not the police will respond, how quickly they will respond, and how many police officers will be dispatched.

Nonetheless, a survey of published research on the police reveals that there has been practically no research on the process determining the mobilization of police resources. A review of the sociological literature discloses that while Reiss and his students (see especially Black, 1968) have pointed to the importance of these decisions, they have devoted their attention primarily to the patrol function and to police/citizen relations in face-to-face encounters. The now classic study by Cumming et al. (1965) seems relevant at first sight. However, this study in fact concerns itself with the nature of police work in the field and not with police mobilization. The study reported by Bercal (1970) makes a start in this direction but from the point of view of the process of mobilization this study is restricted in scope. Furthermore, while it provides some information on what action is taken by the police, it tells us nothing about the decision process that produced these actions. More relevant to this latter question is a study by Chance (1970). However, as Chance's research concerns the relations between city services (including the police) and the socioeconomic characteristics of census tracts, his study, while interesting, is at once too general and too macroscopic to be very useful for an understanding of police mobilization.

Turning to the literature of operations research, there is a great deal of concern with the question of police mobilization (see, for example, Larson, 1970). However, these studies are only tangentially concerned with the question of how police officers presently make decisions. Their principal concern is with developing mathematical models which rationalize decisions in terms of a set of goals.

In summary, then, there is a very real lacuna in the literature on the issue of the process of police mobilization. This gap in knowledge has serious implications for an understanding of the criminalization process. While considerable attention has been given to the highly visible question of police/citizen encounters and while there has been some interest in the question of why citizens call the police (see, for example, Ennis, 1967: McNaughton-Smith and Spencer, 1970) the crucial question of the processing of these calls has been more or less ignored by sociologists. The research described below examines this issue.

The location for this study was a Canadian police department with approximately 4,500 police officers. In this department, all calls for police assistance are eventually processed at the communications bureau, although these requests may be channelled via police divisions if citizens call a division directly. The processing of calls for service is divided into two functions: the complaint function and the dispatch function. The complaint function involves the receipt of calls for police assistance, the decision to dispatch a car, and the recording of the relevant information. The dispatch function involves the selection and dispatch of a patrol car. This function controls the decisions which determine response time and the strength of the response. The officers responsible for the complaint function will be referred to in this paper as complaint officers, and those responsible for the dispatching of patrol cars are referred to as dispatchers. Complaint officers send messages to the dispatchers requesting the dispatch of a patrol car on a card via a conveyor belt.

Data collection for this study involved the following:

1. All calls received at one complaint desk (there are eight in total) were tape recorded for 33 shifts (11 of each of the three eight-hour shifts) over a period of about three months.

2. This provided a total sample of about 6,000 recorded telephone calls. From this 6,000, a subsample of 1,080 calls was randomly selected for analysis.

3. For each of these 1,080 calls the message cards (complaint card) completed by complaint officers were drawn from police files.

4. During each fieldwork session while calls were being recorded, an observer was present in the communications bureau. This observer listened to the calls as they were being taped, and made notes. A principal focus of these notes was the talk by complaint officers either among themselves or with the observer. These fieldnotes constitute the "qualitative" data for the study.

The tape recorded telephone calls and the complaint cards provided the raw data for the "quantitative" analysis. The information from the calls and cards was coded on a variety of dimensions (totalling 89). This material forms the basis for the computer-assisted statistical analysis.

As the analysis of the process of police mobilization remains incomplete at the time of writing, the findings reported in the remainder of this paper must be regarded as partial, tentative and preliminary.

Further analysis may well require the modification of conclusions and interpretations reached at this time.

In the analysis to follow attention will be restricted to the complaint officer's decision to dispatch or not dispatch a patrol car in response to a complaint.

Complaints received by the communications bureau can be roughly divided into two classes in terms of their source: complaints that reach the communications bureau indirectly via police divisions, and calls that reach the complaint officers directly from citizens. Only calls received directly from citizens are considered here, as they alone involve a decision as to whether or not to dispatch a patrol car. In the case of calls received from police divisions, the complaint officer accepts the fact that a decision has already been made at the division by the officer who received the complaint, and therefore he simply passes the message on to the dispatcher. In this sample, 47% of the calls reporting trouble were received by complaint officers directly from citizens. Of these, 18% did not result in the dispatch of a patrol car.

I will begin with a consideration of those complaints for which a patrol car is dispatched and attempt to show that, from the complaint officer's point of view, the crucial question as he defines it is not "should I dispatch a patrol car?" but rather "can I in this particular case, risk not dispatching a patrol car?"

One of the first things noted by the observers during the field-work was the apparent inconsistency between the value and attitudes of many officers as these were expressed in their conversations about calls, and their decisions vis à vis the dispatch of a patrol car. In these conversations many officers indicated that they felt that the public badgered them with a whole host of troubles that were not police troubles (trouble where police intervention was not appropriate). Yet very often officers dispatched a patrol car to trouble which they indicated they did not regard as police trouble. The answer to this puzzle is to be found in formal normative order that officers felt constrained their actions. The complaint officers were aware of this apparent discrepancy between "word and deed" (Deutscher, 1966) and frequently provided the observers with accounts. [3] An utterance that captures nicely the essential features of these accounts is the phrase, "You have to take calls at face value." In the context in which these accounts were heard by observers, they were interpreted as follows: Officers perceive themselves as constrained by a formal normative order. That is, complaint officers are oriented to a set of formal rules within the communications bureau which, among other things, specifies how these officers should respond to citizen calls for police assistance. The rules as they apply to the dispatch of a car can be summarized very simply: "You must dispatch a car in response to every citizen request for assistance." In short, in terms of the formal normative order, as this was perceived by complaint officers, these officers had no discretion with respect to citizen calls for police assistance.[4]

This formal rule was offered by complaint officers to account for their action of dispatching a patrol car, and can be used by analysts for the same purpose. This analysis of the puzzle created by the apparent discrepancy between officers' words and deeds carries with it a subtle irony. For what one finds is that the authoritarian, quasi-military structure of the police department has the democratic consequence of placing the decisions about the allocation of police resources primarily in the hands of the public.[5]

However, while this formal rule solves one analytic problem, it creates another. For if in terms of this rule one can account for the 82% of cases where a patrol car was dispatched, as action which is rule-guided, this analysis leaves the problem of accounting for the deviant 18%.

I would like to begin the consideration of this question by noting that a normative order is felt to be constraining only if it is enforced. Where the normative order has been internalized, enforcement becomes a matter of conscience which takes the form either of self-satisfaction or guilt. On the other hand, where the normative order is not internalized, enforcement takes the form of sanctions which have their origin outside the individual. For many of the complaint officers in the communications bureau, the formal rule was clearly not internalized. In fact, some officers felt quite strongly that this was not a very sensible rule.

Given the above argument, one can conclude that the formal rule usually was felt as constraining by complaint officers only on those occasions when officers anticipated that their actions might be reviewed in terms of this rule. While it was acknowledged by complaint officers that very few of their decisions would in fact be reviewed, as these decisions were but one step in a sequence of future and only vaguely foreseen events, the possibility of a review always existed. This possibility was something that complaint officers took into account in making decisions. However, while complaint officers were always aware of the possibility of their decisions being reviewed, they were also oriented to the "fact" that the probability of a review differed from call to call. This probability was seen by officers to depend on such factors as the power of the caller to initiate a review and the type of call (different types of calls were seen to have different typical future outcomes associated with them).

In estimating the probability of a review, officers relied on their folk knowledge of how reviews typically come to take place, given specific types of calls and specific types of callers. Information about these two questions was, of course, gathered by officers during the call.

However, officers felt constrained as to the questions they could ask as they felt the questions had to be clearly relevant to the topic at hand, namely, the provision of police assistance. Thus, for example, officers felt they could ask a caller where he lived but not about his social status. This meant that in estimating the caller's power to initiate a review, the complaint officer had to rely on information provided in the call either in answer to relevant questions or provided voluntarily by the caller. Given this, officers used both address and the caller's manner of speech as important sources of inference in estimating a caller's potential power to initiate a review.

To account for why officers decide not to dispatch a car, one must note that the degree to which officers feel constrained by the formal normative order differs from call to call. However, the fact that the formal normative order is not seen as constraining by officers in certain incidents does not account for their behavior on these occasions. It simply means that the formal normative order is not an important factor in these decisions. That is, these decisions are not guided by the formal rule. On the basis of the fieldwork, it appears that two factors are of principal importance on those occasions when the formal normative order is not important: the informal value system, and the complaint officer's practical circumstances (Garfinkel, 1967), particularly the perceived "busyness" of the dispatchers.

The essential feature of the value system is that the police officers feel that the public seeks police intervention in connection with trouble that is very often not "really" police trouble. That is, for some classes of trouble complaint officers feel that the citizen's selection of the police as a troubleshooter is inappropriate and that the complainant should have taken care of the trouble himself or have gotten somebody else to "do something about it." Given this belief, one would expect the proportion of calls receiving and not receiving a patrol car to differ for different types of calls, as indicated in Table 7.1. Furthermore, in each category, the proportion of calls that did not receive a patrol car is consistent with what one would expect on the basis of the complaint officer's informal values and folk knowledge about the typical character of various types of troubles.

In this sample, both "suspicious circumstances" and the "report of damage" classifications resulted in the dispatch of a patrol car 100% of the time. The "suspicious circumstances" category comprises such troubles as "signs of entry to building," "report of alarm ringing," "signs of entry to an automobile," "prowlers" and "suspicious vehicles" while the "report of damage" category is made up of "assaults" and "willful or malicious damage to property." These are viewed by the complaint officers as crime troubles (that is, trouble which is very likely to involve a violation of the criminal law) and therefore are, from the point of view of the officers, by definition, police troubles.

TABLE 7.1

Decision to Dispatch Patrol Car, in
Different Categories of Trouble

Type of Trouble	Patrol Car Dispatched		Patrol Car Not Dispatched		Total
	n	%	n	%	
Suspicious circumstances	28	100	0	0	28
Thefts/robbery	34	90	4	10	38
Damage to persons property	13	100	0	0	13
Disputes	36	80	9	20	45
Accidents/emergencies	76	91	8	9	84
Traffic/parking complaint	22	85	4	15	26
Public nuisance	36	91	7	9	43
Service	17	90	2	10	19
Other	21	42	29	58	50
Total	283	82	63	18	346

However, one would expect that "thefts" would also be regarded by the police as crime troubles for "thefts" is made up of such clearly criminal incidents as "robbery" "holdup" "theft of auto," "from auto," "shoplifting," and the like. The fact that patrol cars are not always dispatched to "thefts" despite their criminal nature is accounted for by two features of the officers' folk knowledge of "thefts." First, that many thefts are regarded as criminal but trivial, and further as "something the police can't do anything about anyway." With calls of this sort, a typical strategy used by officers is to convince the caller of the uselessness of reporting the theft, and thereby encourage him to withdraw his report. This is a very appropriate strategy because it allows the officer to refrain from dispatching a patrol car without actually violating the formal rule. Secondly, the police feel that in the case of criminal matters about which they can do nothing in terms of either apprehending the offender or retrieving the stolen goods, they are being exploited by insurance companies who require a police report if insurance claims are to be honored. This sentiment is typically expressed with the phrase "we're just working for the insurance companies."

At the other extreme, there is the category "other" where more than half the incidents reported did not result in the dispatch of a patrol car. This category is made up of a mixed bag of incidents that have in common only the inability to fit into the classification system. The latter was constructed on the basis of the categories used by complaint officers in describing types of trouble, whereas these "other" cases do not fit the scheme of typifications used by complaint officers. While it is clearly false to argue that because an incident fits a routine typification used by the police, such an incident is perceived by the police as police trouble, it is, I suggest, reasonable to assume that the reverse is true. If the police do not have a classification for an incident, then it is unlikely that the incident will be considered by them to be an instance of police trouble.

Turning to "disputes," the police acknowledge that while police intervention is sometimes required, they claim that in many cases it is not necessary. Whether it is appropriate to seek police intervention does not depend so much on the nature of the dispute but rather on what has been done before.[6] This is especially true of "domestic disputes" which constitute 55% of the "dispute" category. Specifically, complaint officers feel that domestic disputes are essentially private troubles which should be settled either by the parties concerned or by friends or relatives, and not by the police. Only after an attempt to settle the matter privately has been made and has proven unsuccessful should police intervention be sought.

In addition there is another element to complaint officers' folk knowledge of "domestic disputes" relevant to the analysis; namely, that these disputes are "known" to be dangerous. For this reason complaint officers are reluctant to dispatch a patrolman to domestic disputes.

The categories "traffic/parking," "nuisance," "service" and the subcategory "property damage traffic accidents" have in common with some "thefts" the fact that complaint officers treat many of these troubles as rather trivial, and therefore as a waste of police time and resources. Nevertheless, they recognize that they are formally required to dispatch a car in response to all complaints. Here again, a typical strategy used by the police is to attempt to persuade the caller of the triviality of the trouble in the hope that he will retract the request for police intervention.

The traffic/parking category presents new element in complaint officer decision-making: a suspicion of busybodies. Complaint officers are suspicious of callers who phone up about someone else's trouble, where there does not seem to be any good reason for them to be acting on behalf of that other person. With busybodies, officers look for ulterior motives. A common motive inferred to busybodies by officers is vindictiveness. This busybody interpretation is typical of certain parking complaints: for example, the complaint that someone is parking on the "no parking" side of the street or that a car has been parked in one spot beyond the legal limit of three hours.

With "nuisance" calls, in addition to the feeling that many of them are trivial, there is the further element that the complaint officers believed that many could be settled privately and, therefore, there was no need to call the police. This is particularly so with noise complaints, which comprise 65% of the "nuisance" category. The complaint officers often regard police assistance in the "service" category as quite legitimate and an essential part of police work; for example, when a hospital requests police assistance in transporting a human organ for transplant from one hospital to another. However, there are many cases in this category that officers regard as blatant examples of the public's exploitation of the police. It is here perhaps more than anywhere else that one finds officers getting annoyed with callers, and consequently it is also here that one is most likely to witness an outright refusal to dispatch a car: "No ma'am I will not send you a car. This is not a taxi service." At this point, the officer terminates the call.

Finally, there is the "accident" category. This class of complaints includes three subcategories: "property damage traffic accidents," "personal injury traffic accidents," and other "medical emergencies." Complaint officers regard the last two categories as legitimate police trouble, so that there is no conflict here between the formal rule and their informal values. However, in the case of "property damage traffic accidents" (which make up 75% of the "accidents" category), while police acknowledge that these events are technically (that is, legally) police trouble, they feel that this is simply another example of the department working for insurance companies. However, there is often a built-in and legal way out, as the police are only legally required to attend "property damage traffic accidents" if the estimated damage is over $200. The feeling of many of the officers, however, is that this figure should be much higher. A noteworthy feature of calls reporting property damage traffic accidents is that they fairly often lead to arguments between the complaint officers and the callers. These arguments arise primarily because the caller claims he cannot estimate the damage, the officer insists on an estimate, and an argument ensues.

The preliminary analysis presented in this paper is based on a study of police decision-making in only one setting. However, I suspect that many features of this analysis can be generalized to the police decision-making in other settings.

Notes

1. Trouble is used here to mean "something wrong that something needs to be done about." This is very similar to the use of the term by Emerson and Messinger (1972). However, the usage here is

more general than theirs, in that it is not restricted to moral troubles, that is, deviance and includes such events as a person collapsing in the street.

2. The person to whom the trouble is taken (Emerson and Messinger, 1972).

3. The term "account" refers to a linguistic device used to bridge a gap between action and expectation (Scott and Lyman, 1968).

4. This analysis is consistent with the finding of Black (1970) that in face-to-face police/citizen encounters police values are not good predictors of officer's actions.

5. See Black (1970, and Black and Reiss (1970) who note that the single most important predictor of the police disposition of incidents is the preference of the complaint.

6. See Buckner (1970) who develops this idea in his analysis of police strategies for coping with troubled situations in which they have intervened, in terms of a typology of levels of social control: primary, secondary and tertiary.

References

Becker, H. S.
  1963   Outsiders: Studies in the Sociology of Deviance. New York: Free Press.

Bercal, T. F.
  1970   Calls for police assistance. American Behavioral Scientist, 13: 681-91.

Black, D. J.
  1968   Police Encounters and Social Organization: An Observational Study. Doctoral dissertation, University of Michigan.

  1970   Production of crime rates. American Sociological Review, 35: 733-48.

Black, D. J., and A. J. Reiss, Jr.
  1970   Police control of juveniles. American Sociological Review, 35: 63-77.

Buckner, H. T.
  1970 The Police: The Culture of a Social Control Agency. Doctoral dissertation, University of California at Berkeley.

Chance, T.
  1970   The Relations of Selected City Government Services to
           Socioeconomic Characteristics of Census Tracts in San
           Antonio, Texas. Doctoral dissertation, University of Texas
           at Austin.

Cumming, E., I. M. Cumming, and L. Edell
  1965   Policeman as philosopher, guide and friend. Social Problems,
           12: 276-86.

Deutscher, I.
  1966   Words and deeds: Social science and social policy. Social
           Problems 13: 233-54.

Emerson, R. M., and S. L. Messinger
  1972   A sociology of trouble. Paper presented at Society for the
           Study of Social Problems.

Ennis, P. H.
  1967   Criminal Victimization in the United States: A Report of a
           National Survey. Washington, D. C.: Government Printing
           Office.

Garfinkel, H.
  1967   Studies in Ethnomethodology. Englewood Cliffs, N. J.:
           Prentice-Hall.

Larson, R. C.
  1970   On quantitative approaches to urban police patrol problems.
           Journal of Research on Crime and Delinquency, 7: 157-66.

McNaughton-Smith, P., and M. Spencer
  1970   First steps in an empirical study of the nature of real and
           imaginary crime. Paper presented at the Fourth Inter-
           national Congress on Criminology, Madrid.

Reiss, A. J., Jr.
  1971   The Police and the Public. New Haven, Conn.: Yale
           University Press.

Reiss, A., J., Jr., and D. J. Bordua
  1967   Environment and organization: A perspective on the police.
           In David J. Bordua (ed.), The Police: Six Sociological
           Essays. New York: Wiley.

Scott, M. B., and S. M. Lyman. Accounts. American Sociological
Review, 33: 46-62.

Stinchcombe, Arthur L.
1963   Institutions of privacy in the determination of police
administrative practice. American Sociological Review,
69: 150-60.

8

RECIPROCAL SUSPICION, SIDE ONE: THE POLICEMAN'S PERCEPTIONS OF MINORITIES
Roger Baldwin

Theoretical Perspective

"Why are you looking at me that way?" "What way?"
"You know what way."

How often have we heard the above conversation, or participated in a similar one ourselves? We take it as a matter of course that when we think we know someone well, we know what he thinks, and we become doubly irritated when we are responded to with a confused or defensive reply. Our certainty of our understanding in these situations magnifies our irritation; our irritation triggers our ensuing behavior. The targets of our irritability can attempt to deny, explain or move away from us, still heightening our anger, or they can agree. If they agree, their own anger will be internalized for the sake of temporary surface harmony, or they may agree in some fewer instances because they see and believe what we seemed to see in them. Obviously, there are more chances for misunderstandings than for understandings to occur in these situations (see Laing et al., 1966).

Bierstedt (1970: 468) contends that where the differences between people are great, conflict is slight; where the differences are slight, there is a tendency to magnify them and hence conflict is great. Many times people may magnify the conflict situations when they assume the differences to be slight. Frequently, there are significant differences in the socialization processes of seemingly similar people that create glass walls or invisible barriers to mutual understanding.

Claiming a working class background, as the police most often do (that is, being raised in the ghetto or the fringe of it and partici-pating in similar child experiences in the streets, schools, or churches) does not eliminate ethnic, national heritage, racial or familial differences and all the many nuances within their configurations. For those who remain socially and culturally within the boundaries of their wider original heritage and for those whose adult life patterns expand into the wider society's ways, their perceptions of each other's ideas and the meaning of each other's behavior become distorted.

It is less of a social problem for people who claim to be or are separated by social class distance to distort their perceptions of each other, than for those who claim to share to any extent social class similarities, since in the second instance actual contact and potential for conflict is greater than in the first. They are prone to make many more assumptions about each other than those who are socially distant. The police as well as minority people exemplify the second type and are guilty of wide misperceptions. This leads to misunderstanding, hurt, and suspicion.

Source of Data

The data for this paper comes from part of a wider project developed to ascertain the policeman's self-image through a series of depth interviews, structured only by several open-ended questions. The interviews were conducted in 1970 and 1971. The respondents were recruited from a single department located in a medium-size city of approximately 100,000 population. The force was made up of about 170 men. Several important factors are involved in the selection of the respondents and in the method of gathering the information.

Much public opinion about police in the United States is based upon experience with exceptionally large metropolitan departments with complements of a few thousand to over 30,000 men. Yet the average city in the United States above 25,000 population has a complement ranging from 15 to 238 men.[1] The city selected for study is therefore more reflective of the average than the extreme cases often cited.

As an instructor at the police academy, I am known by most of the men in the department. Many had themselves urged that a study be done, and were confident that their anonymity would be preserved if they talked freely. Letters were sent to over 75% of the members, patrolmen and rank alike, and more than half responded by coming in for an interview lasting from one to three hours. All were interviewed at the same office and by the same interviewer in order to decrease the probability of differences in responses due to different physical settings or different interviewing techniques.

At a training session for police officers from departments scattered throughout the eastern section of the state where the above department is located, I submitted the series of questions from the study to several volunteer respondentents. Their responses were similar to those of the men in the department studied.

The Police and the Black Community

Skolnick (1967: 80) makes a cogent introduction to the theme of police and black community relationships:

> In principle, the Westville and Eastville Police Depart-
> ments, like most in America, are racially unbiased. That
> is, one would not find in a training manual the idea that
> Negroes should be treated differently in the criminal
> process than whites, nor even that Negroes are apt to
> exhibit greater criminality than whites. The explicit
> principle is racial equality. Yet from the point of view
> of the Negro in America, most policemen—Westville and
> Eastville alike—would be regarded as highly racially
> biased.

With few exceptions, both patrolmen and brass in the present study, in their initial statements, reflected the theme expressed in Westville and Eastville, "We treat everybody alike." The policeman resents any implication that differential or preferential treatment would be given because of race, social class, or any other reason. In fact, it is significant that he initially rejects any form of social class categorization of people in his community. Nevertheless, for whites, he creates his own classifications. Categories such as lower, middle, and upper are replaced with "poor people,""bums or welfare chiselers," "a few big-shot rich people," "and the rest are like me." For blacks, he substitutes, "the older families-good people (they have lived here a long time)," "migrant trash," "and the rest are like me." His major separation for all people in the community is between the "good people" and the "bad ones." They are those who like and respect the police, and those who dislike and are disrespectful, respectively.

The policeman does not see inconsistencies in his attitudes. Although he rejects general social class and racial categorization, he creates his own, highly subjective and prejudiced stereotypes. When the policeman claims that "we treat everybody alike," he has incorporated into his ideas about people one or another relatively superficial similarity that he shares with members of each social class level, white or black. Once this is established, he can simply divide his fellow men into "good guys" and "bad guys." For lower-class people he generalizes similarity in the area of place of residence:

"I was brought up in the same section of town." For the middle class he refers to occupation: "They have to work hard just like me." For the upper class he must reach out with: "They're people too." Although the policeman believes that he has now equalized all people to a single level and therefore deals with them equally as either "good guys" or "bad guys," this level of reasoning is superficial and his predisposition toward interaction with them is not based upon it. As Sagarin (1971: 12) points out:

> It must be made clear, axiomatic as it may sound, that to say that two things are similar in some respects (hence belong to the same category and are described by the same label), never implies that they are identical, nor even that they are alike in any other way than expressed by virtue of inclusion under the given rubric.

The policeman in the present study, after comfortably establishing his own social class divisions, categories which are descriptive rather than composed of technical jargon (which he rejects), proceeds during the interview to eliminate the wealthy black as nonexistent and thus not relevant for discussion. As he says, in confirmation of the Bierstedt principle of social distance, "If there are any [wealthy blacks], they don't bother me." (Actually, there are no wealthy blacks in the city studied, and only a few prosperous, management-level blacks).

The blacks comprise a little more than 1% of the population of this medium-sized city, and with few exceptions reside in a single geographical area. When he gets intensely involved in his discussion of the blacks, the patrolman makes little distinctions between class symbols, such as more expensive homes and better occupations. Whether they keep the homes clean and neat, home ownership and steady employment are paramount considerations for him. After all, neat homes, home ownership and steady employment all indicate responsible, nice people who create few problems for him, he assumes. He sees only a single neighborhood of blacks. As he uses the term "blacks" only sparingly and in public, it is more accurate to say that he sees only "niggers" or "jigs."

Boyley and Mendelsohn (1969: 68) contend:

> Negroes do not enter into nor walk away from contact with the police indifferently. On the contrary, it is terribly significant for them, and they learn from it. It does affect their perceptual world.

The police do not enter into contact with the black indifferently, either. Policemen are highly suspicious of all people. This is a built-in characteristic of their profession. They are especially suspicious of blacks. Why?

Earlier, it was noted that where the differences are slight there is the tendency to magnify them and create conflict. The policeman came out of the same neighborhood, went to the same school, and probably fought in the same school yard as the black. His family was just as poor as the black's is now, especially if he was a child during the Great Depression years. In these respects the differences are assumed to be slight. Here, there is a sharing of the "poor kid" background. If we take the Sagarin axiom into consideration, although in the dominant characteristics they are alike, the magnification of differences are elaborated and exaggerated. Now racial, cultural and religious differences loom large. The policeman is a member of the white majority (consisting of minorities of the past—and present), and the blacks are a minority group. The policeman conveniently over-looks the fact that he is quite often from the dominant national stock in his city and was raised with a particular cultural heritage (mainly German, in this study). He simply sees himself as American. The blacks, with their "soul food" and separate cultural patterns, are highly different from him. Soul food is different. African clothes, hair-dos and names, or gaily colored or extremely fashioned clothes are different, as is black music. Police know it, and blacks reaffirm that there are major differences with the resounding cry, "Black is beautiful."

The policeman considers himself an astute judge of people. He know that his job calls for quick analyses of troublesome situations and troublesome people, and he sizes up social types (or stereotypes) routinely. On the one hand, since he shares the dominant character-istic of "poor kid" background, he assumes he understands the black. On the other hand, as he sizes up the differences in what he observes of blacks in that "same" environment and assumes he further under-stands them, his perceptions become distorted. The ways and the meanings of blackness and black behavior are foreign to the white policeman, thus causing his suspicions of blacks to be greater than those of the whites.

It is important to note that the policeman's prejudgments or prejudices may not be significantly different from those of the general public. He may, as in the case of the white population, even know many of the standard explanations given for the depressed lot of the black American in the United States, and be sympathetic or hostile. What places him in a unique position is that he is in an occupation which calls for contact with blacks more often than most other jobs whites are in, and that he meets blacks most frequently in stressful circumstances. The most critical point is that with heightened suspicion and negative expectations, his predisposition is to act in a hostile manner toward blacks and treat them with less genuine consideration than he would whites.

Police officers whose assignments bring them into frequent contacts with minority people form more intense attitudes toward them, pro or con, but even a pro attitude is a basically weaker, negative one than a purely favorable one which they might hold toward members of the white majority. It would seem that the greater contact is not the key to decreasing suspicion (Boyley and Mendelsohn, 1969: 66). An officer expressing a pro position reported that "most of them [blacks] are pretty good people. I never had no [sic] trouble with them. They toe the line in your presence but they stick together." For this officer, although he expresses a positive position, his suspicion of blacks as a group is reflected in the key phrases "in your presence" and "but they stick together." Another patrolman assigned to the same area complained bitterly "that those wise militants demand their rights and openly challenge you." Still another sneered, "I have no use for them." Then he added, as he looked directly at the interviewer, "but then, I have no use for lazy whites either." Once he had established equal treatment as his stated pattern, as indicated in his comment about whites, he went into a tirade about a black who had "beat up his own crippled mother and stole her welfare checks." From that point on there was no attempt on his part to cover up his contempt and distrust of blacks.

Most of the brass reported favorable opinions of the blacks. Frequently, they would comment that the majority of blacks have respect for law and order and think that the local police are "o.k." They are, for the most part, socially distant from blacks by virtue of their positions in the department. As was true of some patrolmen, the brass spoke quite favorably about the older black residents. "It is the younger black or the migrant that agitates," or "Thank God that the older people keep us posted." One command officer spoke with great praise about the blacks' [good sense in the] treatment of him when he was called to quell a potential riot of about 100 blacks assembled in the streets.

Beyond the glowing statements about cooperation of the blacks, one gets such generalized comments as, "I read if over 5% of the blacks are troublemakers, you have a good chance of a riot." "I pity them." "They have a deep-rooted animosity for us."

The brass are also more apt to talk at length about their resentment of legislation which they feel favors the blacks more than the patrolmen. They do not usually interact with blacks and do not hold as intense feelings as the line officer out on the street.

Other Minorities

The analysis of the police and the black minority must suffice as the prime example of all police-minority relationships. One way to summarize the relationship of the police to the other minorities, however, would be to note that as "blackness" or "blackways" are foreign to the white policeman, so too are the Spanish language of Puerto Ricans and other Latins. Similarly foreign to the police are the ideas, ideals, and appearance of such minorities as rebellious youth and morals offenders (Baldwin, 1970). While these groups are on the one hand foreign to the policeman, on the other hand he assumes that he understands them and, within this contradiction, he resents them and is suspicious of them.

It would seem that greater contact with minority people is not the key to decreasing suspicion. Greater awareness of the differences and of the meaning of those differences for minority peoples can decrease the policeman's hostility, suspicion, and predisposition to act negatively toward them.

Note

1. According to Uniform Crime Reports for 1969, there were some 49 cities over 25,000 in population in Pennsylvania, with police forces of 15 to 238 persons. This did not include Philadelphia, with a force of 8259, and Pittsburgh, with 1776. There were 243 cities with less than 25,000 inhabitants, with police forces ranging from 1 to 34 persons.

References

Baldwin, Roger
    1970   The police as morals enforcers. Paper presented to annual meeting of Pennsylvania Chiefs of Police.

Bierstedt, Robert
    1970   The Social Order. New York: McGraw-Hill.

Boyley, David H., and Harold Mendelsohn
    1969   Minorities and the Police: Confrontation in America. New York: Free Press.

Laing, R. D., H. Phillipson, and A. R. Lee
    1966   Inter-Personal Perception. New York: Springer Publishing.

Sagarin, Edward, ed.
1971   The Other Minorities. Waltham, Mass.: Ginn and Co.

Skolnick, Jerome H.
1967   Justice Without Trial. New York: Wiley.

9

PERCEPTIONS OF POLICE
LAW ENFORCEMENT PRACTICES
IN NEW YORK'S PUERTO RICAN
GHETTO, "EL BARRIO"
Wayne L. Cotton

An increasing crime rate and a recurrence of civil disorder
are two major problems which affect all elements of our society and
all of our major institutions. At an operational level these problems
most directly involve the members of ghetto communities (comprising
a number of different minority groups in our society) and the police.
These minority communities are involved so deeply because it is here
that increasing crime takes its major tool, and that social and racial
tensions, pressures for social change, and civil disorders are largely
concentrated. Since the police are the instrument of control and enforcement in the society, they are the most directly involved in these
processes on a day-to-day basis.

For a variety of reasons, methods of policing such communities
have, in the majority of cases, proved inadequate. These methods
have not protected the residents from the climbing crime rate nor
have they given them a sense of security either in their homes or in
the streets. There is little doubt that the abrasive nature of police-
community contacts in the ghetto areas is at least partially responsible
for the inadequacy of police protection, and that an improvement in
the attitudes on both sides is a necessary step in any overall improvement of the situation. The problem is especially critical because of
the feeling among ghetto residents that police treatment of them is
much worse than of other segments of the general public, and that
they in particular are often singled for police brutality and harassment. Christopher Rand (1958:58) states that an especial amount of
hostility is felt by New York Puerto Ricans toward the police, often
as a result of police tactics.

There have been a number of studies, most of which have come
to the same conclusion: that ghetto residents do not like the police,
and that the police return the compliment in their attitudes and actions.
Citizens complain that the police are neglectful of their duties, unfair,

and too preoccupied with minor crimes to be efficient in solving major ones. The latter belief is attested to by Kadish (1967) concerning the entrapment policies of many police departments in enforcing laws against "vice." Even though there are increasing numbers of minority group members in urban police departments, they are often viewed by ghetto residents at best as misled and at worst as servile "lackeys of the establishment."

A study, conducted by Toro Calder, Cedeno and Reckless (1968) in Puerto Rico, found negative attitudes toward the police. Although this study was formulated to obtain attitudes of prisoners, guards and police as well as of laborers, it proved useful in indicating the widespread negative feeling that is directed toward police and law enforcement.[1]

But while most research has indicated a strong dislike for police, it has often not gone further and examined in more detail some of the root causes of such negativism. For example, are the police themselves seen as the culprits, or unfair laws which they impose? Could the feelings against the police be changed by different police procedures? Do ghetto residents want no police around at all, or do they simply want better police? Has antagonism gone so far now that even improving police service would be to little avail in changing attitudes in the community? Such questions apply especially to the younger members of the community because they are usually the most articulate in expressing their views, and because they will shortly be the leaders and spokesmen of these communities.

There have been studies, on the other hand, that have indicated a much more positive appraisal of the police in some ghetto areas, or more positive than would be imagined from the unfavorable publicity that police-community relations have recently received in such communities. The President's Commission on Law Enforcement and Administration of Justice (1967), for example, found a generally high regard for the police among all groups studied, including black men, who felt that the police do not get enough credit or support for the community.

A Baltimore study for the Office of Economic Opportunity (Wallach and Carter, 1971) suggests that the residents of the black ghetto have an essentially positive orientation toward the police, albeit with considerable ambivalence, and would welcome more rather than less interaction with the police officers who patrol their communities. However, they would like such interaction to be more personal and reciprocal than at present, and would expect the police to modify some of their present behavior patterns.

The present study shows an essentially negative appraisal of the police in El Barrio. This may perhaps be summed up (much as Rand, cited above, has observed) by the attitude that the police pick on Puerto Ricans more than on other groups in the city. In fact the responses to a direct question to that effect elicited the belief among the sample population that police treat Puerto Ricans worse or even much worse than any other group, by a margin of more than two to one. In any case, it is obvious that the police suffer much criticism, which often becomes a "damned if they do, and damned if they don't" type of situation. And there are suggestions that the most negative attitudes of all toward the police are held, not be minorities, but by upper middle-class whites. Nevertheless, whatever the truth of that assertion may be, one returns to the central problem of the role of the police in regard to the ghetto communities.

One of the most important factors in this regard is the type of community in which the police have to operate; i.e., does the community represent a lifestyle that is similar to that of most police who work there, or does it differ radically from it? In this respect, Banton (1964:180) indicates that there are reasons to believe that many police prefer to work in lower-class neighborhoods since the middle-class areas provide less of a challenge (and perhaps less chance for promotion), and are in many cases "boring beats." On the other hand, it cannot be denied that ghetto areas are likely to be more dangerous for the police, and the inhabitants less cooperative than in middle-class precincts.

How far such a difference in values and outlook between police and a community affects law enforcement is a debatable but important point. In an article in the New York Post of May 13, 1972, the question of assigning an all-black force to Harlem was discussed; evidence indicated that a considerable percentage of the community would welcome such a move. David Riley (1969), in discussing community control of police, seems to think that such control may be the only workable solution short of violence.

Wayne LaFave (1965) demonstrated the dilemma of police justification in taking account of the local mores in deciding whether the process of enforcement should be invoked against a member of the particular community. LaFave indicates that, in his observation, there are many variations in enforcement from place to place, attributable in part to differing public attitudes in various locales.

William F. Whyte (1965) brings up the point of public relations and police behavior as a major problem in enforcement, and the image of the police and the law itself. If often becomes a question of class or ethnic values to which the policeman does not subscribe. The public need and demand for protection of a professional nature is also a most important variable in the whole process of enforcement; if the community sees the policeman as an interloper, he can hardly do an efficient job, and such feelings on the part of the public can cancel positive aspects of the legitimate demand for protection. Establishment of efficient law enforcement depends on a desire and a demand on the part of community residents for that type of service. Nothing less will do (Banton, 1964:1).

It would seem that one way to solve the conflict in values between police and community would be to assign more patrolmen of the same racial and ethnic background to ghetto neighborhoods, and indeed this procedure has been demanded by various militant groups. Most police departments do not subscribe to the view that this would be desirable or help very much in law enforcement, and many citizens interpret it as just another form of racism in reverse. The respondents for the present study did not support this approach either, as only some 30% felt that assigning more Puerto Rican policemen to their community would notably improve the quality of law enforcement. The general comment was that, in any case, such police would still be representing the "system," although it was admitted that an ability to speak Spanish would be a distinct advantage.

The police, on the other hand, have another viewpoint on the problem of enforcement. According to Skolnick (1966), they are very cognizant of the problem of community relations, although they seem to emphasize different factors than does the general public. For example, the police felt that lack of respect, lack of cooperation, and lack of understanding of themselves were the greatest difficulties, while the public in ghetto communities placed racism and lack of understanding of different values as most important. Police usually did not mention racism in the first rank of problems, and this omission may be interpreted variously as: indifference to the feelings of minorities, avoidance of the issue, or a simple refusal to discuss what is considered a delicate matter.

In order to examine some of the attitudes from the community side of the question of law enforcement and police behavior, the present research examines the attitude of residents of one ghetto community in New York City, East Harlem or "El Barrio." While there are considerable numbers of other minority groups—mainly blacks, but with some Italians and a few others—the area is largely populated by Puerto Ricans. Whereas in many areas of the country it is primarily the blacks who see the police as oppressors and as victimizers of their group so far as brutality, corruption, and other related social ills are concerned, in New York the Puerto Ricans see themselves in that position or, in the opinion of some, in an even worse position.

The population of respondents used in the present study was composed of young Puerto Rican males between the ages of 18 and 30. A considerable number of these were migrants from Puerto Rico, with the expected language and cultural difficulties, but the majority were born and reared in New York, able to cope with conditions in the city, and often very articulate. Those respondents were interviewed by bilingual interviewers using a questionnaire designed to test some of the attitudes toward police and their activities in law enforcement. The final sample consisted of 230 respondents.

The area of El Barrio is one of the most congested parts of the city, with almost no home ownership and very high absentee ownership of buildings and businesses. Housing ranges from the very worst kind of outmoded tenement with just bare essentials, and sometimes not even those, to a large number of public housing projects, which while providing much better physical facilities, are often overcrowded and in many cases heavily crime-ridden. Narcotics use and sale is an ever-present problem to the residents of this area. In other words, it is a typical inner-city ghetto area, with all the accompanying problems.

For purposes of making comparisons, the respondents were divided into three categories according to level of acculturation. That is, those who were born and reared in New York, speak English fluently, and have considerable social contacts with non-Puerto Ricans, among other variables, are considered as highly acculturated. Those who are fairly recent migrants, speak little English, and restrict their lives mostly or entirely to other Puerto Ricans, are considered poorly acculturated. The third category of the moderately acculturated consists of those respondents who are at neither extreme and who have a somewhat marginal existence between the two worlds. It was expected that these three groups would have significantly differing perceptions of the police and so it turned out, but not wholly as anticipated.

In asking questions in this area, several different factors were probed. These include: the law itself and its fairness, general police image, police efficiency, and police method of operation. It is obvious that all of these do not have to be either positive or negative. For example, one might feel that the police are efficient, but deplore the method used to obtain that efficiency. Or, the law might be seen as basically fair, but the way in which the police carry it out looked on as unfair.

The results indicate that very few of the respondents, only about one in five, feel that the law is usually fair. This would indicate that in El Barrio there is much dissatisfaction with the law itself, as well as with its method of enforcement. In addition, about half of the respondents thought that the police did not enforce the laws strictly enough, but the reasons for this were not so much support of the law itself as the belief that police do not take action against the really serious violators, or play favorites, or get involved with payoffs and bribes. The consensus appears to be that by strictly enforcing the laws, the police would make themselves more honest as well.

In considering the overall police image, the negative opinions become even more obvious. A good indicator of attitude would be an appraisal of the honesty of the police. In the present sample only about one-third of the respondents believe that the police usually are honest, and more than one in five feels that they are almost never honest. An even stronger indictment is shown by the fact that 35% feel that police are just as bad as the criminals.

In like manner, police efficiency is doubted to a large extent, as shown by the belief that police do not do a good or efficient job, with almost half (45%) saying that their performance is poor or very bad. None believe that the police perform very well, which contrasts markedly with official proclamations of how the police show restraint and skillfully perform in the face of vast difficulties, especially in dealing with trouble in ghetto areas. The residents of El Barrio simply do not think this is so. Nor do they believe that the police are especially efficient in apprehending criminals, since 55% indicate that they think the police do not usually arrest those who commit serious crimes. About the same proportion believes that the police waste a great deal of time on petty criminals and minor violations. The negative opinions of efficiency are not so widespread as of the police image. This may indicate that the people are willing to tolerate some inefficiency rather than run the risk of overzealousness on the part of the police, which could be considered more of a danger to the average citizen.

Police methods of operation are also looked on with a great deal of negativism. Like the overall image, this aspect of police work seems to arouse more emotion than efficiency per se. The overwhelming majority believe that police are brutal from time to time, and almost one third (30%) think that brutality occurs often. About the same proportion feels that police respect the rights of suspects rarely or never, and a large majority (80%) feels that police are not sufficiently careful before arresting innocent persons.

In spite of all this negativism, two interesting findings emerge. These are that somewhat over 50% of all respondents agree that having more police on the job would be desirable, and just about the same number think that the police should be paid higher salaries for dangerous work. While this may appear contradictory to all that has just been stated, it is not necessarily so, because there is much evidence that the respondents feel that higher salaries and greater police coverage would increase their professionalization and make them more cognizant of the community's problems. They definitely want police protection, and do not feel that they are getting it.

Further observations can be made regarding the three levels of acculturation into which the respondents were divided. With few exceptions, both the poorly acculturated and the highly acculturated had similar views, while those more marginal had differing views, and these latter were more often positive in their appraisal of the police than the other two categories of respondents. It had been thought that the least acculturated individuals would give the poorest ratings to the police and the most acculturated persons would rate them higher.

Summary

The overall picture that emerges from these findings is that the police have a very bad image in Spanish Harlem. These respondents feel that the police do not like them and treat them very badly; they also believe their methods of operation to be questionable at best and brutal at worst, and their efficiency open to much improvement. In spite of these attitudes, a small majority feels that things would be better if there were more police, and that the police ought to receive higher salaries. It would seem obvious that the residents of El Barrio do not entirely reject the concept of the police as a social force, and would probably welcome better police services. They do, however, seriously object to the police as presently constituted and do not have much faith in either their methods or their efficiency. But to say, as some have done, that the police must go, or that no matter what changes are made, the ghetto will never accept the police in any way, is not borne out by the attitudes expressed here.

The level of acculturation of these respondents is related very definitely to the favor or disfavor with which they view the police, with those who are relatively little acculturated indicating the most negative opinions. However, while it had been expected that the most acculturated respondents would show the most positive attitudes, such was not the case. Rather it is those in a more marginal status, the partially acculturated, who indicate greater approval and support for the police and the law. In many ways, the poorly and well acculturated individuals are closer to each other in their attitudes than either is to the partially acculturated.

It appears somewhat difficult at first sight to explain the reasons for this finding. It might be expected that with increased socialization toward the general American culture, individuals would come to accept the police as representatives of the law and give them greater support. While this does occur, it does not manifest itself to anywhere near the degree expected. One possible explanation relates to the marginal status of the partially acculturated Puerto Rican. A possible analogy might be found in the situation of social classes in the general society. According to many polls, news reporting, and sociological analysis, the middle-class American, and especially the lower middle-class individual, is most insecure about his status, both economically and socially. The "law-and-order" philosophy gets its strongest support from that segment of the population. While this, like most analogies, leaves much to be desired, it is quite possible that the only partially acculturated member of society—in this case the Puerto Rican—feels most keenly his marginal status, and is somewhat confused about the place he occupies both in relation to his own ethnic group, and the larger society. In a sense, the better acculturated Puerto Rican has "made it"within the larger society, and is somewhat more secure in his self-image, while the least acculturated person is still trying to cope with just existing and is likely to feel the full brunt of discrimina tion by the society at large, even his own people perhaps, and most especially by the police. In other words, the moderately acculturated person is trying very hard to be accepted and to find a place in the total culture, and may become somewhat ritualistic in his views of social institutions and their representatives.

The main reason, perhaps, why the most highly acculturated respondents may have such negative opinions of the police could resid with their better education and a greater awareness of just what ghett law enforcement entails. While they may not personally feel the brun of discrimination and bad police practice to the extent that their less acculturated brothers do, it may rankle them even more because of their awareness. They are able to analyze what is happening, and to develop very intense feelings of resentment and hostility toward those who are making it difficult for "their people." These same individuals may also feel somewhat guilty about their better fortunes than many others in El Barrio, and react with stronger attitudes.

One implication that this study brings out is that increasingly these young, better educated members of the ghetto communities are going to have to be dealt with. This evidence supports the opinions voiced by youth leaders and social workers familiar with ghetto prob- lems. Their attitudes are going to be increasingly the ones that count and any plans for future police-community relations will have to take them into account. A practical consideration derived from the reality of these trends would seem to indicate a policy of trying to bolster and reinforce the realization of identity of ethnic groups and to make it a useful force in strengthening law enforcement in the whole society What many leaders—and interestingly, the most acculturated among them—in the Puerto Rican community are calling for is a recognition of and respect for their Hispanic culture and identities, and this is being stressed in ways never attempted by earlier immigrant groups.

Other possible areas for research in this area could include studies of police attitudes toward Puerto Ricans, similar to those done by Skolnick and LaFave. It might be useful to know if the police make distinctions, and if so, what kind of distinctions, according to their perceived level of acculturation of individuals with whom they have to deal. The matter of police discretion in making arrests in Puerto Rican ghettos could also prove informative. In addition, further information concerning the young, better educated Puerto Ricans, who are often in the vanguard of the more aggressive assertions of "Puerto Rican Power," would prove useful in formulating the types of reforms necessary or practical in law enforcement.

Note

1. I am indebted to the authors of this research, especially Dr. Reckless, for permission to use a number of the questions used by them in the present study, and for insights into the problems of phrasing such questions to elicit more valid responses.

References

Banton, M.
  1964   The Policeman in the Community. New York: Basic Books.

Kadish, S. H.
  1967   The crisis of overcriminalization. Annals of the American Academy of Political and Social Science, 374: 157-70.

LaFave, Wayne
  1965   Arrest: The Decision to Take a Subject into Custody. Boston: Little, Brown.

New York Post
  1972   Should Harlem Be an All-Black Beat? May 13.

President's Commission on Law Enforcement and the Administration of Justice
  1967   Public attitudes toward crime and law enforcement. In Task Force Report: Crime and Its Impact, an Assessment. Washington, D.C.: Government Printing Office.

Rand, Christopher
  1958   The Puerto Ricans. New York: Oxford University Press.

Riley, David P.
  1969   Should communities control their police? Civil Rights Digest, 2(Fall): 26-35.

Skolnick, Jerome H.
  1966   Justice Without Trial. New York: Wiley.

Toro Calder, Jaime, Cerefina Cedeno, and Walter C. Reckless
1968   A comparative study of Puerto Rican attitudes toward the
        legal system dealing with crime. Journal of Criminal Law,
        Criminology and Police Science, 59: 536-41.

Wallach, Irving, and Colette C. Carter
1971   Perceptions of the police in a black community. In Study
        for Office of Economic Opportunity. McLean, Va.: Rand
        Analysis Corp.

Whyte, William F.
1965   Street Corner Society. Chicago: University of Chicago
        Press.

10

**SEXUAL DEVIANCE AND
LAW ENFORCEMENT:
DILEMMAS OF POLICE POLICY
REGARDING VICTIMLESS CRIMES
OF SEXUAL DEVIATION**
Emilio C. Viano

With the dramatic increase of crime in the past decade, police
agencies across the nation are under pressure to account for the use
of their resources. At the same time, the United States has experienced a kind of sexual revolution brought about by several interrelated
factors and, most importantly, from a police standpoint, by a new code
of obscenity law, made possible by a number of United States Supreme
Court decisions. These decisions have resulted, for example, in films
being exhibited across the nation that clearly portray acts of sexual
deviation that are prohibited by law. Certain groups in society, such
as the Citizens for Decent Literature, assert that these films are
obscene on their face because of the portrayal of unlawful conduct.
Prosecution of the films on this ground or other grounds, however,
has been relatively unsuccessful because of the criteria laid down
in the Supreme Court's Roth decision of 1957 and in a number of
opinions rendered since the Roth decision.[1] In the plurality opinion
in the Court's decision of Memoirs v. Massachusetts,[2] the Justices
require what amounts to a three-part test for judging "obscenity":

(1) The dominant theme of the material taken as a whole appeals
to a prurient interest in sex; (2) the material is patently offensive
because it affronts contemporary community standards relating to
the description or representation of sexual matters; (3) the material
is utterly without social redeeming value.[3] This is still the basic
test for obscenity, although there have been other decisions that have
increased First Amendment rights in this area. The most important
of those in reference to police role and policy in victimless crimes
is Stanley v. Georgia,[4] handed down in 1969. In this case the court
ruled that an individual has the right, protected by the First and
Fourteenth Amendments, to read or observe what he pleases in the
privacy of his own home even though the material involved is obscene.[5]

Contemporary community standards may be the key element in this new outlook on sexual matters, and should be carefully considered by the police in the formulation of policy in victimless crimes. For example, in an obscenity trial in the Superior Court of the District of Columbia, the presiding judge remarked, in reference to evidence the government had presented outlining its view of community standards, that "twenty years ago if a young lady of eighteen was absent from her home unchaperoned over a weekend she was most likely to be severely admonished by her parents upon her return; today, the parents would not blink an eye over the episode." The appearance of topless dancers that began in California and spread across the country, and the opening of numerous "gay" bars in several major cities where persons of the same sex dance with one another, are further evidence of the change occurring in the public's attitude toward sex.

In 1966, the Supreme Court in Ginzburg v. United States[6] added a pandering requirement on the Roth test for obscenity. This ruling took into account the manner of distribution of alleged material. For material to be obscene it must be advertised in a way so as to assault individual privacy, making it impossible for an unwilling person to avoid exposure to it. On the basis of this case, in January of 1972, a judge in the Superior Court for the District of Columbia found a defendant not guilty of a charge of Committing an Indecent Act in an amusement arcade that featured "peepshow" films of a sexual nature. The judge reasoned that anyone entering the arcade, due to its nature, knew what to expect and therefore could not be offended by a display of nudity on the part of the defendant. He also made reference to the several "topless" dancers that had been operating arrest-free for some time. However, the judge noted, the type of conduct occurring in these locations would be justification for arrest if it were to occur in public with unwilling individuals present.[7]

The Problem

These examples of judicial conduct typify the changes of attitudes among the public which make it possible to extend the First Amendment rights. Thus, the police are faced with a dilemma in the formulation of policy[8] regarding victimless crimes of sexual deviation for two reasons:

(1) An increasing crime rate along with a decreasing tax base in most large cities makes it difficult to increase the number of policemen; thus the need to account for the use of the existing resources; and

(2) The relaxation of community standards toward sexual conduct which is evidenced by the difficulty in obtaining convictions in cases

that a few years ago were handled routinely. The problem is further heightened by the Ginzburg and Stanley decisions that imply that conduct which does not intrude upon an unwilling individual and occurs in private between consenting adults is their own affair.

Methodology

To examine this dilemma, I will research current laws relating to victimless crimes of homosexuality and prostitution as they apply to adults, since it is within these areas that the majority of police manpower is utilized in matters of "vice." Police operational policy is considered, as it exists in the Metropolitan Police Department of Washington, D.C. While this places some limitations on the paper, the policy of the Washington police department is probably reflective of other cities in the 500,000 to 1,000,000 population range. Included will be interviews with a judge, police supervisors, and representatives of a deviant sexual group.

Laws and Policy

A foremost problem that the police claim to face in the area of victimless crime enforcement is the law. For example, in the District of Columbia the most frequently used law for street prostitution is a solicitation charge. For the prostitute to commit this offense, she must state to the undercover officer that she is willing to engage in a sexual act for a price. Of course, the experienced prostitute is aware of this requirement and attempts to pull the proposition out of the prospective customer, thus nullifying any solicitation on her part. Some prostitutes have resorted to requesting that prospective "car tricks"[9] display their penis, feeling that a police undercoverman would not be permitted to go that far. Requesting identification and patting down a prospective customer are additional means employed by the prostitute to verify that she is not dealing with the police.[10] Thus for the police to arrest prostitutes for solicitation, within the law, is quite difficult. The indictment of seven vice-squad officers here for allegedly making illegal arrests and falsifying reports in a number of prostitution cases could be an outgrowth of the futility of the solicitation law.

In past years, the Washington police were more successful in combatting street prostitution with a vagrancy statute that was struck down in the Ricks decision of 1968.[11] This statute permitted a police officer to make an arrest after observing a prostitute on three different occasions attempting to ply her trade. With this law the police could function with far less manpower than required under the solicitation law. While only a few experienced officers were needed for vagrancy, a constant supply of new undercovermen is needed in solicitation, as it is unlikely that a prostitute would solicit the same undercoverman more than once. Adding to the expense of a continuous supply of new undercovermen is further need for innovative methods to fool the prostitute. Locally, the police have resorted to renting expensive automobiles and taxi cabs along with employing various disguises. All this is an expensive proposition forcing the police to face a difficult decision regarding continued allocation of manpower and funds in this area.

Meanwhile, prostitution is on the increase. In the Washington area it is estimated that prostitution increased approximately 300% between 1968 and 1972. The police are blaming it on the Ricks decision and are calling for new legislation. Is this a realistic approach in light of the new attitudes and of the recent court decisions? In February of 1972 the United States Supreme Court struck down the vagrancy statute in Jacksonville, Florida, stating that the law was too vague and "encouraged arbitrary and erratic arrests . . . and places almost unfettered discretion in the hands of the police." Vagrants were defined in the code, among other things, as "lewd, wanton, and lascivious persons . . . persons neglecting all lawful business and habitually spending their time by frequenting houses of ill fame . . ."[12] The FBI Uniform Crime Reports state that 113,400 persons were arrested for vagrancy in the United States in 1970. It would be hard to determine just how many of those arrests were sex-related, but if the District of Columbia is any indication, prior to the Ricks decision, the number would be substantial. For example, there were 168 prostitution-vagrancy arrests there in 1967.[13]

In the case of arrests for homosexual activity, the police fare no better than prostitution with the current laws. The most frequently used law is Disorderly Conduct which is a "collateral" offense. This means that a person arrested can elect to forfeit anywhere from $25 to $100 if he does not wish to contest the case in court. This procedure is the same as for a traffic violation. While there are no specific elements relating to sexual matters in the Disorderly Conduct statutes,[14] other than rude or obscene gestures, these arrests, according to police policy, must have the elements of a more serious charge of Committing a Lewd, Indecent, or Obscene Act which is punishable by a fine of not more than $300 or imprisonment of not more than 90 days, or both.[15] Apparently by charging persons with the lesser offense, the police attempt to keep these cases out of the jurisdiction of the court. The normal collateral for Disorderly Conduct is $10. The police base their authority for taking more than that sum on a collateral list issued by a former chief judge of the Superior Court.[16]

However, upon examination, the Indecent Act statute is vague, and the test of the offense must be obtained from the decisions which generally have placed restraints on how far the officer can go in effecting these arrests. Ironically, in one decision, Rittenour v. D.C.,[17] decided in 1960, the District of Columbia Appeals Court ruled that this section does not apply to an act occurring in privacy or in the presence of a single consenting adult.

To make arrests for homosexual conduct, the police regularly check local men's rooms in department stores and hotels, peepshow arcades, and any other public place where persons are known to loiter for the purpose of engaging in sexual activity. Investigations begin with one officer going into the location to observe the activity while the other serves as a coverman. If an arrest is made, the coverman can then corroborate the offense as far as time, place, and circumstances. This is a requirement stemming from the Kelly v. D.C., and is applicable to all homosexual cases.[18] The question is how much entrapment is involved in this situation, when an act is committed in the presence of a single police officer. Humphreys (1970: 88) in an extensive study of homosexual hangouts, points out that the person who frequents these locations would rarely molest a "straight" or a detective unless that person would first give his consent by showing an erection. He cites a U.C.L.A. study which asserts that if the police play a decoy role in effecting these arrests, then by overstaying the time limit of the "straight" they are engaging in entrapment rather than detection, particularly in light of the U.C.L.A. study finding that

> the majority of homosexual solicitations occur only if the individual appears responsive and are ordinarily accomplished by quiet conversation and use of gestures and signals having significance only to other homosexuals.

This type of enforcement policy then might be seen to foster rather than deter unlawful activity on the part of the police. The police response to this assertion is that they never exceed the time of a "straight," unless they have probable cause to believe that a crime is about to be committed. The question, then, is how long a "straight" spends in a men's room. This is a difficult question to answer and remains subject to the discretion of the officer.

Problems of enforcement in this area are becoming difficult for the police for many additional reasons:

1. The arcade case, which restricts the police to patroling areas where "straights" might be offended.

2. The increasing scrutiny by homosexual organizations, like the Mattachine Society, complaining of arrest tactics employed in

wooded areas of local parks. Spokesmen of these organizations contend that, rather than send young, casually dressed police officers into the parks to make arrests, the police function would be better served by instituting some uniform patrol in the form of crime prevention. However, from a police standpoint, this approach would have the effect of eliminating law enforcement practices generally felt to be superior to ordinary patrol.

3. In December 1971, the Florida Supreme Court struck down the state's 103-year-old "crimes against nature" law, leaving only misdemeanor provisions in effect against homosexual conduct and other deviant acts.[19] In this ruling, the Court said the statute could not meet the constitutional requirement that the language be understandable to the common man. The ruling reversed sentences given to two men who were caught in a parked car by a St. Petersburg policeman who said he witnessed a homosexual act between the two. Ironically, a week before this decision the Florida legislature was awarded an LEAA grant of $46,000 to study the necessity for such laws (Washington Post, 1971).

Effects

Are the laws prohibiting prostitution and homosexuality needed? If control is required, is the police the best agency for the job? An answer to these questions was offered by the Commission Report on Non-Victim Crime in San Francisco (1971). The Commission was funded by an LEAA grant, and its task was to inquire whether it was wise to deploy law enforcement personnel to enforce these areas of public morality while the police had solved only 13% of reported serious crimes in 1969. At the same time, over 50% of all arrests made by the police were for victimless crimes. The Commission hypothesized that to curb crime in San Francisco would entail a greater expenditure over the entire system, or a reexamination of the priorities of law enforcement. In looking at the existing laws in the area, the Commission developed a set of seven principles:

1. The law cannot successfully make criminal what the public does not want criminal.

2. Not all the ills . . . of society are the concern of the government. Government is not the only human institution to handle the problems, hopes, fears or ambitions of the people.

3. Every person should be left free of the coercion of criminal law unless his conduct impinges upon others, injures others, or if it endangers society.

4. When government acts, it is not inevitably necessary that it do so by means of a criminal process.

5. Society has an obligation to protect the young.

6. Criminal law cannot lag far behind a strong sense of public outrage.

7. Even where conduct may be properly condemned as criminal under the first six principles, it may be that the energies of criminal law enforcement are better spent concentrating on more serious things. This is a matter of priorities.

If one can agree with these principles, then the dilemma of the police is in sharper focus.

The Commission in San Francisco found that in 1967 it cost the city more than $270,000 to arrest, process, and prosecute 2,116 prostitutes to the point of sentencing, plus probable jail costs in excess of $100,000 for those who were convicted. The total cost: more than $375,000 or an estimated cost per arrest of $175, a quite high one. In 1969 only 15% of all persons arrested on prostitution charges ended up in jail. In the District of Columbia, the conviction rate was less than 50% in 1971, indicating a revolving-door process— that is, a continuous cycle of arrest and release—with the police giving an appearance of "controlling" prostitution. Of all homosexual arrests in Washington, D.C. from 1966 to 1970, only one defendant is known to have been actually given a jail sentence. During that same period, only a small number of cases proceeded beyond the prosecutor's office, and a majority of those were dropped after the defendant had undergone a period of psychiatric treatment. This policy of the prosecutor seems to be in line with the second principle of the San Francisco Commission.

Police arrests for homosexuality in Washington decreased from 469 in 1960 to 69 in 1968. This indicates that police policy is becoming cognizant of the changing standards in the community. Nevertheless, current official policy still calls for dealing with the problem by arrest. A Task Force on Homosexuality appointed by the National Institute of Mental Health (1969) reported that, while estimates of homosexuality are only tentative, it is believed that there are at least three to four million adults in the United States who are predominantly homosexual. In the area of police enforcement procedure, the Task Force found that entrapment was not uncommon; that existing laws are selectively enforced; and that serious injustice often results. According to the Report, professionals working in this area maintain that the extreme disgrace society has attached to homosexual behavior by way of criminal statutes and restrictive employment practices has done more social harm than good, and goes beyond what is necessary for the maintenance of public order and human decency. This view is consonant with the third principle of the San Francisco Commission.

Blackmail of homosexuals is often a result of police policy in homosexual arrests. This may result from the vagueness of the law and the plainclothes method of investigation. It can be seen that the homosexual is not quite sure of where he stands when he is attempting to make a sexual contact in a public place. He is at the mercy of the plainclothes police officer if he is unlucky enough to have chosen a location patrolled by the police. It is also reasonable to assume that stories of police arrests for these offenses constantly circulate among deviant groups and many have been misrepresented. Hence, such locations are a favorite base of operation for the blackmailer, taking advantage of an individual who is not quite sure of what type of conduct constitutes an offense. The homosexual who is approached by a bogus police officer has little knowledge of whether or not he has really been arrested by the police. On the other hand, the police admit that quite a few individuals resist arrest for homosexual acts, partially because of the plainclothes method used in performing such arrests.

From 1969 to 1971 the police in Washington, D.C. saw a number of suspected homosexuals report to police headquarters on the orders of a phony police sergeant who had contacted them by phone after observing them frequenting homosexual hangouts. It was later learned that if the individual contacted expressed alarm at reporting, he was instructed that the matter would be dropped provided that he send the sum of $2,000 by Western Union to the desk of a downtown hotel where the blackmailer was registered under a fictitious name. Those who reported apparently did not fear arrest, but what of the unknown number who were successfully blackmailed? This suggests that policy in this area should be changed to a preventive function by the use of uniformed patrol, and that this should be made known to the public so that the opportunity for blackmail would be reduced.

Meanwhile, in the area of prostitution, police policy has produced few fruitful results and perhaps has indirectly contributed to increasing the severity of the problem. The contention that enforcing the laws against prostitution is more destructive than the profession itself, that indeed the laws reinforce prostitution and hinder effective law enforcement against the complex of crimes with which it is linked, is often heard. While prostitution arrests in Washington increased from 181 in 1968 to 596 in 1971, arrests for procuring have risen from zero in 1966 to 11 in 1971. The police unit which handles this activity increased from 5 members in 1966 to 18 in 1971.

The San Francisco Commission found that procurers have an enormous leverage on prostitutes working the street. In other words, when there is great risk of arrest a prostitute is in need of someone to supply bail money and assist in obtaining legal counsel. It is known that some "pimps" have lawyers on retainer to handle their girls' arrests. Some are also known to have standing arrangements with bail bondsmen to obtain the quick release of their girls after arrest. The "pimp" then can withdraw these benefits at any time to keep a

dissident prostitute in line. Thus the court processing and bail required
of women arrested for prostitution are among the major factors linking
them to their "pimps." Lacking money, counseling, or alternative
employment, prostitutes have no other choice but to return to their
"protectors" who pay their bail and promptly send them back to the
streets. On the other hand, because of delays in getting a case to
trial, some prostitutes have been known to change a plea of not guilty
to guilty because they fared better.

It is in this complex web of interrelationships that police graft
thrives. The 1971 Knapp Commission findings in New York City are
only the best known in a series of disclosures of police collaboration
with prostitution. It is also contended that the laws are applied against
streetwalkers but rarely affect call girls. This selective law enforcement promotes disregard for the legal system and lends weight to the
feeling that the law and its enforcement are biased according to class.

Suggestions for Reform

The San Francisco Commission recommended that discreet off-
the-street prostitution activity cease to be criminal in an attempt to
reduce street activity. This would not only reduce the need for the
"pimp" to exist and operate, but would also eliminate the confidence
game activity that flourishes with heavy street activity. This is in
the form of the "murphy" game where a confidence man without prostitutes promises to obtain one for a customer who is then instructed
to place his money in an envelope which the confidence man exchanges
for another containing either play money or cut newspaper. In come
cases, this activity has led to violent robbery when the customer
realized what was happening and attempted to back out of the proposition.

The police sometimes argue that their techniques represent the
only way of enforcing the existing laws. This statement can be used
as an argument for statutory reform. Careful examination of police
resources and capabilities reveals that the police are not well equipped
to handle successfully certain forms of social deviance, including
homosexual conduct and prostitution, with the consequence that more
effective legislation or a transfer of responsibilities should occur.
Would the public welfare be endangered by moving the problem into
the hands of more appropriate community agencies? Apparently it
would not, based on the analogy of the transfer of public drunkenness
cases from police "drunk tanks" to medical and social centers, such
as detoxification centers.

In response to changing views on sexual matters and to court
decisions, the police should discontinue the plainsclothes or undercover

arrests of homosexuals and prostitutes. The police are losing ground in this area. Theirs is almost an impossible task. Future police involvement in the area of homosexuality and prostitution should be primarily in the form of uniform patrol, focusing on prevention rather than detection. This policy should be announced to the public and would have the immediate effect of beginning to reduce some of the problems that the existing policy has fostered, such as: (1) the blackmail and adverse mental effects on homosexuals, as pointed out by the NIMH Task Force Report; (2) the pressure on police officers who are required to effect these arrests under most difficult circumstances; (3) most importantly, the need for the police officer to be the complainant or the offended party in homosexual arrests (it is difficult to understand how a police officer who is employed to visit homosexual haunts can be offended by a display of sexual conduct on the part of a defendant). This new policy would permit the police to reallocate needed manpower and funds into other areas of greater public concern, and would have the added effect of relieving the workloads of the prosecutors and the courts.

Notes

1. Roth v. United States, 354 U.S. 476 (1957).
2. Memoirs v. Massachusetts, 383 U.S. at 413 (1966).
3. 383 U.S. at 462.
4. Stanley v. Georgia, 394 U.S. 557 (1969).
5. 394 U.S. at 568.
6. Ginzburg v. United States, 383 U.S. 463 (1966).
7. Interview with Judge Charles Halleck, Superior Court of the District of Columbia, April 3, 1972.
8. "Policy" as used in this paper refers to operational policy rather than stated policy and means an accepted procedure, methodology, or a settled course of action.
9. Customers who seek out prostitutes from their automobiles.
10. Interview with supervisory personnel, Prostitution and Perversion Branch, Metropolitan Police Department, Washington, D.C., March 24, 1972.
11. H.M. Ricks v. District of Columbia, 414 F. 2nd 1097, 134 U.S. App. D.C. 201 (1968).
12. Papchristuv et al. v. City of Jacksonville, 40 U.S.L.W. 4216 (U.S. Feb. 29, 1972). Vagrancy statute in Jacksonville, Fla. para. 26-57; Fla. Stat. para. 856.02.
13. Metropolitan Police Department, Washington, D.C., Prostitution and Perversion Branch Records.
14. Title 22, Section 1107 of the D.C. Code.

15. Title 22, Section 1112 of the D.C. Code.

16. Interview with supervisory personnel, Prostitution and Perversion Branch, Metropolitan Police Department, Washington, D.C., March 24, 1972.

17. Rittenour v. D.C., D.C. Mun. App., 163 A. 2d. 558 (1960).

18. Kelly v. D.C., D.C. Mun. App., 139 A. 2d. 512 (1958).

19. Fla. Stat. para. 800.01 (1971) amending Fla. Stat. para. 800.01 (1957).

References

Humphreys, Laud
    1970   Tearoom Trade: Impersonal Sex in Public Places. Chicago: Aldine.

National Institute of Mental Health
    1969   Final Report of the Task Force on Homosexuality.

Report
    1971   A Report on Non-Victim Crime in San Francisco. Part II. Sexual Conduct, Gambling, and Pornography.

Washington Post
    1971   December 20.

11

A TYPOLOGY OF
POLICE CORRUPTION

Julian Roebuck and
Thomas Barker

This paper postulates an empirical typology of police corruption derived from a content analysis of the literature (1960-1972) and the police work experience of one of the authors. Police corruption is analyzed as a form of organizational deviance hinging primarily on informal police peer-group norms.

The vast content of the literature deals with value-laden accounts by muckraking journalists and the confessions of exposed police officers Messick, 1968). The few articles and occasional selections appearing in scholarly journals and books are based on case study methods of ex-officers' confessionals about criminal activities (Stern, 1962; Stoddard, 1968). Behavioral scientists, who have engaged in the participant observation of the police, have paid scant attention to police corruption per se, though several have furnished sketchy accounts (Skolnick, 1966; Westley, 1970).

We define police corruption as any type of proscribed behavior engaged in by a law enforcement officer who receives or expects to receive, by virtue of his official position, an actual or potential unauthorized material reward or gain. Behaviors defined as police corruption transgress contradictory normative systems: (1) violations of formal police departmental administrative rules and regulations, (2) violations of informal operating norms, (3) violations of criminal laws.

Typology of Police Corruption: Dimensions of Study

Police corruption occurs within a number of specific (corrupt) patterns, each of which is analyzable along several dimensions: (1) acts and actors involved; (2) norm violations; (3) support from the peer group; (4) organizational degree of deviant practices; and (5) police department's reactions:

1. There are at least two actors involved in most acts of police corruption, a corruptor and the corrupted officer.

2. The acts may involve violations of formal department norms, or legal norms, or a combination of these two.

3. The support and degree of support that acts of corruption receive from the peer group will vary from act to act, with the identity of the violator and the corruptor, informal peer group norms, and the situational context of the violation. For example, in a number of acts involving "clean" money, the group may offer overt or covert approval. Actually, some types of police corruption are seldom considered deviant, and may be considered appropriate within certain situational contexts. In some police departments anyone not engaging in these "deviant acts" would be considered deviant. Frequently, acts involving "dirty" money are considered deviant by the group. We view the peer group as a microcosm of the organization and assume that sustained peer group support of certain corrupt acts reflects organizational support. This assumed organizational support does not imply that all police organizations wholeheartedly approve of any or all corrupt police practices; however, most police administrators privately admit that the eradication of all types of corrupt police practices is impossible. Police administrators are really concerned with how much and what types of corrupt police behavior should be permitted (Niederhoffer, 1969: 176).

4. Acts of corruption differ according to their organizational context.

5. Police department's reactions depend upon type of corruption, identity of the violator and corruptor, situational context of the violation, informal policy of the organization, and public disclosure of the act and actor. Reactions fluctuate from indifference, acceptance, condonation, administrative adjudication, and disposition to criminal prosecution.

Eight Types of Police Corruption[1]

Corruption of Authority. The officer's authority is corrupted when he receives officially unauthorized, unearned material gain by virtue of his position as a police officer without violating the law per se. Ostensibly, the officer receives free meals, booze, commercial sex, free admissions to entertainment, police discounts on merchandise, services, or other material inducements "just because the corruptor likes the police." Additionally, rewards which violate departmental rules and regulations include payments by businessmen to police for property protection beyond routine patrol duties; secret payments by property owners to police for arresting robbers and burglars at their establishments; payments by bondsman bounty hunters to police for the arrest and notification of bond jumpers.

The corruptors are "respectable" citizens, "showing their gratitude for efficient police work." Acceptance of gifts and gratuities often marks the first step in the conditioning of an officer into other types of police corruption (Stern, 1962:99).

Corrupt acts of this sort are usually defined as violations of departmental regulations but not as violations of criminal statutes. It is likely that most police peer groups support these gratuities ("goodies") which they do not define as corrupt when received from noncriminals of high status (Niederhoffer, 1969:177). Officers might rationalize these gifts as informal rewards deserved because of their low pay and hazardous working conditions. Officers in some police departments who refuse to accept gratuities are considered deviant by their peer group.

Many police departments, though publicly disavowing this behavior, accept it as a system of informal rewards. Informal organizational policy usually condones these unorganized practices, and reaction is likely to vary from acceptance to mild disapproval.

Kickbacks. In many communities police officers receive goods, services, or money for referring business to towing companies, ambulances, garages, lawyers, doctors, bondsmen, undertakers, taxicab drivers, service stations, moving companies, and others who are anxious to sell services or goods to persons with whom the police interact during their routine patrol (President's Commission, 1967: 208-9). Corruptors are usually legitimate businessmen who stand to gain through a "good" working relationship with police officers. Kickbacks violate formal departmental norms but are not generally defined or acted upon as criminal violations.

The peer group may support kickbacks from legitimate businesses as "clean" fringe benefits earned by virtue of their position. Many officers who refuse all kickbacks are labeled deviant by some peer groups. The degree of peer group support depends on the following contingencies: trustworthiness, reputation, status, and affluence of the corruptor; adeptness of the corruptor in presenting his rewards as "clean" money; and the secrecy of the situation.

Kickback organization inheres in the collusion between businessmen and policemen. Businessmen distribute cards to police indicating their willingness to transact business. Some arrangements must operate in the determination of payments to the policemen who make the referrals.

Many departments either condone or overlook kickbacks so long as the corruptor is a legitimate businessman, the officer is otherwise acceptable to the department, the value of the goods and services is held to a minimum. Most departments react negatively to cash kickbacks. The condonation of kickbacks depends on the following situational contingencies: informal definition of "clean" money, discretionary and secrecy measures utilized by corruptor and corrupted, the status and reputation of the corruptor. In communities where such working agreements are traditional, the police establishment may offend the legitimate business community by strong overt reaction. Reaction varies from acceptance to mild sanctions in the case of goods and services; cash kickbacks may result in stronger disciplinary action, i.e., suspension or dismissal.

Opportunistic Theft: From Arrestees, Victims, Crime Scenes, and Unprotected Property. These acts do not involve any corruptor. Rolled arrestees, traffic accident victims, violent crime victims and unconscious or dead citizens are generally unaware of the act (Messick, 1968:151). Officers investigating burglaries may take merchandise or money left behind by the original thief. Officers may also take items from unprotected property sites discovered during routine patrol; e.g., merchandise or money from unlocked businesses, building materials from construction locations, unguarded items from business or industrial establishments. Finally, policemen may keep a portion of the confiscated evidence they discover during vice raids, e.g., money, booze, narcotics and property. All of these behaviors violate departmental and criminal norms.

Peer group support depends upon the peer group's informal policy of accepting or rejecting "clean" money, the definition of "clean" money (the smaller the amount of money and the smaller the worth of the article taken, the cleaner the money) and "dirty" money, and the situational umbrella of secrecy. Most police departments react negatively to this opportunistic and unorganized type of theft. Reaction is usually contingent upon: (1) the department's informal definition of "clean" money, (2) the value of the theft, (3) public exposure, and (4) the willingness of the victim to prosecute. Sanctions vary from mild disapproval, admonitions and warnings to suspensions, dismissals, and criminal proceedings.

Shakedowns. Shakedowns arise opportunistically, i.e., the officer inadvertently witnesses or gains knowledge of a criminal violation and violator and subsequently accepts a bribe for not making an arrest. The corruptor may be a "respectable" citizen who offers a bribe to an officer to avoid a traffic charge, or a criminal adventitiously caught in the commission of an illegal act who induces the officer to free him. Shakedowns violate both departmental and criminal norms.

Officers who take bribes from transporters of contraband such as gambling paraphernalia, bootleg liquor, or money from traffic violators are not considered deviant among peer groups who draw

121

distinctions between "clean" and "dirty" money. Even officers not engaging in any form of corruption are likely to maintain a code of silence about these acts. On the other hand, taking bribes from certain kinds of felons, e.g., narcotics pushers, burglars, or robbers is considered deviant by most police peer groups. The situational contingencies that determine the susceptible officer's actions related to shakedowns include: the trustworthiness, reputation, status, and affluence of the victim; the victim's front and presentation of self; and the umbrella of secrecy that covers the negotiating circumstances.

Departmental reactions to shakedowns fluctuate with the definition of and the informal policy toward "clean" and "dirty" money. Most departments, even those open to other types of corruption, react negatively to shakedowns. Departments that tacitly condone shakedowns are concerned with the selectivity of the victim, e.g., transporters of contraband, out-of-town drivers, and low class, powerless citizens are often considered fair game. Publicly exposed officers are usually heavily sanctioned, e.g., dismissal and/or criminal proceedings.

Protection of Illegal Activities. Corruptors are actively engaged in illegal conduct and seek operation without police harassment. So-called victimless crimes (frequently in violation of unenforceable laws) including vice operations pertaining to gambling, illegal drug sales, prostitution, liquor violations, abortion rings, pornography rings, homosexual establishments, and after-hours clubs frequently involve police-protected enterprises (Schur, 1965). Legitimate businesses operating illegally also pay for protection; e.g., some cab companies and individual cab drivers pay some police officers for the illegal permission to operate outside prescribed routes and areas, to pick up and discharge fares at unauthorized sites, to operate cabs that do not meet safety and cleanliness standards, and to operate without proper licensing procedures. Trucking firms pay for the privilege of hauling overloaded cargoes and driving off prescribed truck routes (Smith, 1965:148-50). Legitimate businesses may also pay police officers to avoid Sunday "blue" laws (Burnham, 1970a:18. Construction companies may pay police officers to overlook violations of city regulations, e.g., trucks blocking traffic, violating pollution guidelines (burning trash, creating dust, etc.), destroying city property, blocking sidewalks (Commission to Investigate Alleged Police Corruption, 1971:5).

Regular operation of all the above enterprises indicates police collusion with illegal operators, and most of these enterprises function within criminal organizations. These collusions and conspiracies break both formal departmental and criminal norms.

Peer group support depends on the peer group's policy of accepting or rejecting "clean" money; the trustworthiness, status (position, respectability, influence, prestige, authority, and power in the underworld and/or upperworld) and affluence of the corruptor; and the situational facility of secret and secure transactions (Skolnick, 1967:207-8). Police who receive protection money as well as many community members view this type as a necessary, regulated, patterned evasion; i.e., a publicly accepted norm is covertly violated on a large scale with the tacit acceptance or approval of the same society or group, at least as long as such corruption is concealed (Reiss, 1966). Though the community may desire the illegal services and goods regulated by protection money, officers (even those not on the take) who fail to enforce the law in this area are compromised and corrupted by their inaction. Contrariwise, those officers who attempt to enforce unsupported laws which sanction "protected" goods and services may be thwarted; e.g., arrestees are freed because of insufficient evidence; small fines and/or sentences are dispensed; judges and prosecuting attorneys chastise and discourage officers for "overzealousness" in this area; cases are quashed or nolle prossed. This dilemma functions to drive many honest and dedicated police officers to resignation, ritualism, inaction, or corruption. Moreover, community approval of "protected" illegal goods and services militates for a thoroughly deviant and criminal police organization.

A high degree of organization is usually present in this type. For successful protection, several members of the police organization must know what places, businesses, and persons enjoy immunity; systems of ongoing communication must be insured; payoffs and police protection must be negotiated. Protection of illegal vice operators may be so complete in some departments that officers who inadvertently arrest "protected operators" must pay a fine to the corrupt officers who have illegally licensed the vice operators (Burnham, 1970b: 9). Protection money also requires illegal routinized departmental procedures and sanctions against uncooperating operators varying from arrest to murder (Time, 1972:22). There is usually a distribution of payoffs with all members of vice details receiving prorated shares of the action. Officers transferred from lucrative vice details to less desirable (in this case, less profitable) assignments often continue to draw for a specified time their former share of the protection money as "severance pay" (Dougherty, 1972:6). Protection money organization may resemble an interlocking bureaucracy as a suborganization representing the police and organized crime. The degree and extent of organization in this type of corruption may (and often does) penetrate and include other municipal governmental institutions (Gardiner, 1970).

Departmental reaction hinges on the degree of its involvement with criminal organizations or "legitimate businesses" that operate illegally; informal definition of "clean" money; identity of the corruptor;

and public disclosure of the violations. If department involvement is deep and widespread, exposed and publicly identified officers will usually be allowed to resign as quietly as possible in order to prevent any large-scale investigation. On the other hand, should strong pressure for sanctions be exerted by legal systems without the police organization, the disclosed officers would probably be dismissed and criminally charged. Sanctioned officers usually accept their fate as an illegal occupational hazard. Those who "sing" are rarely able to support their "song," i.e., supply sufficient evidence to invoke indictments of their peers or supervisors who are also receiving protection money.

Police departments with informal policies that condone the acceptance of protection money attempt to block investigations by any persons, groups, or organizations—at times with the aid of criminals or other corrupt legal systems. Aid may take the form of physical violence against person or property or "devious legal" and/or administrative procedures within or without the police organization.

The Fix. Two sub-types constitute the fix: (1) the quashing of prosecution proceedings following the offender's arrest; (2) "taking up of" traffic tickets. Corruptors are arrestees attempting to avoid court action, and citizens seeking to avoid blemished driving records. The fixer in criminal cases is often a detective or some other designated police officer who conducts or controls the investigation upon which the prosecution proceedings are based. The investigating officer may agree to "sell the case," that is "withdraw prosecution." In criminal cases, the investigating officer either fails to request prosecution, tampers with the existing evidence, or gives perjured testimony. The case may be sold directly to the criminal by the investigating officer or negotiated by a go-between. In some police departments, it is even possible to fix homicide cases and felonious aggravated assaults against police officers (Buckley, 1971:44).

The traffic ticket fixer may be the ticketing officer who subsequently agrees to dispose of the ticket for a fee. Contact with the fixer may be made directly by the citizen or by a designated go-between. Other police officers who have control of the traffic ticketing process at any time after the original citation may fix tickets.

The fix violates departmental and criminal norms. Peer groups overtly oppose the sale of felony cases; however, a frequent conspiracy of silence in some police departments lends covert support to officers who engage in this activity. The selling of misdemeanor cases and the fixing of traffic tickets is not as seriously frowned upon by those peer groups that accept "clean" money.

In many departments where criminal cases are fixed, the operation is highly organized; e.g., some groups of professional or organized criminals maintain a "payroll of detectives" who are able to fix cases. Occasionally, the fix costs the lives of the corruptors. Some "honest" and self-righteous police kill some professional criminals whom they apprehend at the criminal scene, because they think that the fix is in. The arrest and subsequent conviction of a felon is a major source of prestige among police officers, and many officers legitimate violence against felons as a form of community service, i.e., the means justifies the end (Westley, 1970:129-52).

The departmental reaction to the fixing of criminal cases is generally severe, i.e., dismissal and/or criminal prosecution. Even police departments that condone the fix are likely to sanction severely publicly exposed officers. Reaction to ticket fixing depends on the status, reputation, and influence of the corruptor, the department's informal policy concerning "clean" money, and the secrecy of the transaction. Reaction ranges from acceptance to administrative suspension or dismissal.

Direct Criminal Activities. This type involves no corruptor. Policemen directly commit crimes against the person or property for material gain that are in clear violation of both departmental and criminal norms. These actions receive no support from most police peer groups (not even from peer groups engaged in other types of corruption). Direct criminal activities, e.g., burglary and robbery, are defined as extreme forms of "dirty" money crimes, and those few who engage in them do so at great peril (even from most of their colleagues on the force). Generally, some organization is connected with this type. Groups of police officers operate (e.g., as burglars or robbers) in small working groups similar to the modus operandi of professional criminals (Smith, 1965:15-30).

Departmental reaction is extremely severe. Departments tolerating other forms of corrupt behavior will prosecute and send to prison officers discovered engaging in this type (Wilson, 1970:207).

Internal Payoffs. Internal payoffs regulate a market where police officers' prerogatives may be bought, bartered or sold. Actors in this type, both corruptors and corrupted, are exclusively police officers. Prerogatives negotiated encompass work assignments, off-days, holidays, vacation periods, control of evidence, and promotions. Officers who administer the distribution of assignments and personnel may collect fees for assigning officers to certain divisions, precincts, units, details, shifts, and beats; or for insuring that certain personnel are retained in, transferred from, or excluded from certain work assignments (Burnham, 1970b:18). In departments taking protection money from vice operations, officers may contact command personnel and bid for "good" (lucrative) assignments. Usually, everything else being equal, the profitable assignments go to the highest bidders. Certain off-days and selected vacation periods are sometimes sold by supervisory personnel, e.g., an officer who wishes to be off on the weekend, who wishes to avoid split off-days, or who desires a vacation during peak summer months may pay his supervisor for these privileges. Members of a police department whose prerogatives include the control of criminal evidence (e.g., investigating officers, detectives, evidence technicians, desk sergents) may sell this evidence (e.g., wiretaps, fingerprints, forged documents, contraband, and other physical evidence or instrumentalities of the crime) to an officer who in turn uses it in shakedowns or fixes (Newsweek, 1971). All internal payoffs break formal departmental and criminal norms.

Most peer groups probably do not support this blatant, criminal activity. On the other hand, peer groups engaged in other types of illegal corruption, e.g., protection money, shakedowns and fixes, might accept internal payoffs as necessary and inevitable. Officers in certain assignments have little opportunity to "score" in other types of corrupt activities. Payoffs provide these with an illegitimate opportunity structure. Many peer group memberships oppose internal payoffs which result in their own exploitation and victimization.

Internal payoffs are often highly organized within departments engaged in illegal types of corruption. Departmental reaction varies with department's involvement in other types of illegal corruption, the secrecy of the arrangement, and the willingness of the officers involved to expose and prosecute fellow officers, i.e., from acceptance and protection to exposure and dismissal or criminal prosecution.

Summary

This typology does not infer the universality of one or more types of police corruption. Since norms and rules pertaining to police corrupt behavior are relative and problematic in time and space, the typology will have to be empirically tested, retested and modified accordingly.

The eight types of police corrupt behavior are arranged in a hierarchial fashion from rule breaking to lawless behavior. This arrangement suggests a progressive process in dynamics, accretion, and gravity; a process that might be checked at one or more levels of progression by the tolerance limits of the police organization or the community. In police organizations where several types of corrupt behavior exist, the police department operates in a systematically lawless manner. Although protection of illegal activities has been considered the most prevalent form of police corruption, illegal vice operators and legitimate companies operating illegally find it hard to corrupt a police organization where other types of corruption do not already exist.

Note

1. Type nomenclature is based on modifications of definitions and terms on and about different forms of corrupt police behavior derived from three sources: (1) the literature; (2) patterns of police dishonesty discussed in Chapter 7, "Police Integrity," (President's Commission, 1967:208-12); and (3) participant observation by the junior author while employed as a police officer.

References

Buckley, Tom
    1971   Murphy among the meat eaters. New York Times Magazine, 121(December 19): 44-54.

Burnham, David
    1970a   Graft here said to run into millions. New York Times, April 25, p. 1.
    1970b   Gamblers' links to police lead to virtual licensing. New York Times, April 16, p. 1.

Commission to Investigate Alleged Police Corruption
    1971   Interim Report on Investigative Phase. New York, mimeographed.

Dougherty, Richard
    1972   The New York police. Atlantic Monthly, 229(February): 6-10.

Gardiner, John A.
    1970   The Politics of Corruption. New York: Russell Sage Foundation.

Messick, Hank
    1968   Syndicate in the Sun. New York: Macmillan.

Newsweek
    1971   Cops on the take. 78(November 1): 48-53.

Niederhoffer, Arthur
    1969   Behind the Shield: The Police in Urban Society. Garden City, N.Y.: Doubleday Anchor.

President's Commission on Law Enforcement and Administration of Justice
  1967   Task Force Report: The Police. Washington, D.C.: Government Printing Office.

Reiss, Albert J., Jr.
  1966   The study of deviant behavior: Where the action is. Ohio Valley Sociologist, 32(Autumn): 1-12.

Schur, Edwin M.
  1965   Crimes Without Victims—Deviant Behavior and Public Policy: Abortion, Homosexuality, Drug Addiction. Englewood Cliffs, N.J.: Prentice-Hall.

Skolnick, Jerome H.
  1966   Justice Without Trial. New York: Wiley.

Smith, Ralph Lee
  1965   The Tarnished Badge. New York: Thomas Y. Crowell.

Stern, Mort
  1962   What makes a policeman go wrong? Journal of Criminal Law, Criminology and Police Science, 53: 98-101.

Stoddard, Ellwyn R.
  1968   The "informal code" of police deviancy: A group approach to "blue coat crime." Journal of Criminal Law, Criminology and Police Science, 59: 201-13.

Time
  1972   Chicago cops under fire. 100(July 10): 22.

Westley, William A.
  1970   Violence and the Police: A Sociological Study of Law, Custom, and Morality. Cambridge, Mass.: M.I.T. Press.

Wilson, James Q.
  1970   Varieties of Police Behavior. New York: Atheneum.

III

CRIMINAL JUSTICE
AND THE COURTS

12

THE EFFECT OF
THE OFFENSE AND THE
OFFENDER'S SOCIAL
STATUS ON CRIMINAL
COURT DELAY

Edward Green

The problem of delay in the court has been regarded primarily as an ailment of the civil court and has been conceived largely in terms of the administration of procedural rules governing due process and logistical difficulties stemming from the organization of the court (Zeisel, Kalven, and Buchholz, 1959: xxiv; Rosenberg, 1965: 29-59; Sykes, 1969). The criminal court, however, is not immune to this malady. The increase in criminal cases has imposed staggering caseloads upon the judge, prosecutor, and defense lawyer, and has resulted in the sacrifice of due process for a mass production of dispositions (Barrett, 1956: 85-123).

Although the federal Constitution requires that persons indicted for criminal acts be afforded a prompt trial, the criterion of promptness eludes specificity. A study of metropolitan courts shows that the average amount of time between the date a criminal trial is scheduled and the date of final disposition may extend, depending on the community, from a few days or weeks to 14 months. Whether any particular period of time meets some reasonable standard of dispatch depends upon a variety of factors. Cases differ greatly in the amount of time required for adequate preparation. A lengthy delay in the clearance of a case through the docket may be construed, depending upon the circumstances, as favorable or unfavorable to the defendant. As a disadvantage it may infringe upon his constitutional guarantee of a reasonably prompt trial. As an advantage it accords the defendant his full right to a careful presentation of his case and also yields strategic gains: evidence grows cold, the recollections of key witnesses fade, the complainant may forgive the defendant, or the prosecutor,

This research was supported by a grant from the Walter E. Meyer Research Institute of Law.

burdened by more current and more demanding claims upon his time, may decide to drop the case. The advantage conferred by delay upon the defense becomes conversely the disadvantage of the prosecution. The legal requirement to keep the flow of cases moving at a reasonable rate conduces to an attrition of cases at various procedural levels between arrest and conviction and the informal policy of bargaining for a reduced charge or a mitigation of the sentence in exchange for a plea of guilty. Such outcomes militate against the attainment of the goals and values of law enforcement and create a serious disparity between the law in theory and the law in action.

The burden of disadvantage in lengthy delay, it is widely thought, descends most weightily upon the underprivileged who can least afford to post bail or to retain professional counsel. Thus the poor are more likely to await trial in prison or less likely to reap any of the strategic benefits of delay. In this report, I shall examine the effects of the offense and selected socioeconomic characteristics of the offender upon the length of time elapsing between arrest and disposition. The data consists of all municipal court dispositions during the years 1942, 1950, 1960, and 1965 and all circuit court dispositions during the years 1942 through 1965 originating in arrests made in Ypsilanti, Michigan. Ypsilanti, a small industrial community of 25,000 persons in southeastern Michigan, reproduces on a small scale many of the features of urban growth and development and the concomitant stresses, including very high crime rates, characteristic of major urban centers in the United States.[1]

Defendants charged with ordinary misdemeanors are tried in the Municipal Court of Ypsilanti.[2] Those charged with high misdemeanors and felonies are tried in the Circuit Court, a tribunal of county-wide jurisdiction in Ann Arbor, Michigan, the county seat.

The municipal court, through which passed the cases of over 90% of all persons arrested in Ypsilanti during the four sample years studied, performed with great dispatch, disposing of 82.6% of its cases within three days after arrest (see Table 12.1). A month after arrest only 5.4% of the cases had not yet cleared the docket. The circuit court trying the more serious crimes understandably moved much more slowly. Table 12.1 shows that only 24.6% of the cases had been ajudicated within two weeks of arrest, and only 55.7% of the cases within a month.

The character of the offense significantly conditions the duration of the period from arrest to disposition. The findings suggest that the prospect of strict sanctions in the event of conviction for the more serious forms of offenses conduces to a more thorough preparation of cases and elicits a strategy of delaying tactics. As Table 12.1 shows for the municipal court, which tries nothing more serious than ordinary misdemeanors, cases of crimes against the person or drunken

TABLE 12.1

Percentage Distribution of Categories of Number of Days Elapsed between
Arrest and Disposition, by Level of Court and Type of Offense

Offense	0-3 Days	4-7 Days	8-15 Days	16-30 Days	31 Days and Over	Total N	Total Pct.
Municipal Court							
Person	64.3	5.4	11.6	9.3	9.3	129	100.0
Property	76.8	5.6	4.2	4.2	9.2	142	100.0
Drunken driving	71.6	4.1	1.8	2.4	20.1	169	100.0
Other offenses	84.7	4.0	4.2	3.2	4.0	2433	100.0
Total	82.6	4.1	4.4	3.5	5.4	2873	100.0
Circuit Court							
Person	3.0	1.5	6.8	21.2	67.4	132	100.0
Property	3.3	7.2	18.6	35.6	35.3	334	100.0
Other offenses	4.8	6.4	13.8	30.8	44.2	419	100.0
Total	4.0	6.0	14.6	31.1	44.3	885	100.0

133

driving, involving potentially stricter penalties than other offenses, have the highest proportions of cases carrying over beyond one week after arrest. In the circuit court, also, as shown in Table 12.1, cases of crimes against the person are the slowest to grind through the docket; only 32.6% of all cases were disposed of within 30 days after arrest. Crimes against property go through most quickly: 64.7% were disposed of within 30 days after arrest. The remaining types of crimes, collectively, fall between crimes against the person and crimes against property, with a percentage of 55.8% disposed of within 30 days after arrest.

The problem of delay per se then would seem to be less important than its implications for the delivery of quality legal services to persons of lower socioeconomic rank. Nagel (1965) has observed that in a sample of cases disposed of by state criminal courts, the indigent defendant experienced more delay on the average than the nonindigent defendant. The reason for the variance is uncertain. Conversely, in a sample of federal court cases, the indigent experienced less delay than the nonindigent but, Nagel infers, for not altogether benign reasons: in federal cases the indigent are all represented by court-appointed attorneys who devote less time to the cases or request fewer continuances than private counsel. Whether delay is an advantage or disadvantage in any particular case, I assume for purposes of this investigation that it should occur in about the same degree among the different categories of any social classification provided that the legal process does not discriminate against or favor any particular category. This assumption is tested in Table 12.2 for cases disposed of in the circuit court, using race and occupation as criteria of socioeconomic status.

The circuit court data exhibits no statistically significant differences between white and Negro defendants in the proportion of cases disposed of after time periods of varying lengths. Holding constant the type of offense, observe that Negroes accused of crimes against the person generally wait somewhat longer from arrest to disposition than whites. Twice as many white cases proportionately as Negro cases, 16.0% to 8.5%, are adjudicated within a month of arrest; a fourth again as many Negroes as whites, 73.1% to 58.0%, wait more than 2 months for the disposition of their cases. In cases of property crimes the racial difference declines considerably. White cases are completed more quickly than Negro cases; 30.4% of the white defendants and 26.3% of the Negro defendants wait less than a month; 32.5 and 40.9% of whites and Negroes, respectively, wait more than 2 months. The relative standing of the two races reverses itself in the analysis of the miscellaneous category of other crimes; a slightly larger percentage of Negroes waits less than a month and a slightly

TABLE 12.2

Percentage Distribution of Categories of Number of
Days Elapsed between Arrest and Disposition in
the Circuit Court by Race and Occupation, with
the Type of Offense Held Constant

	0-30 Days	31-60 Days	61 Days and Over	Total N	Pct.
Crimes Against the Person					
Race					
White	16.0	26.0	58.0	50	100.0
Negro	8.5	18.4	73.1	82	100.0
$x^2 = 3.4$; df $= 2$; P $>.10$					
Occupation					
White collar and skilled	0.0	50.0	50.0	4	100.0
Semi-skilled and unskilled	14.9	18.9	66.2	74	100.0
Unemployed	11.1	22.2	66.7	27	100.0
x^2 (combining both categories of employed) .17; df=2; P $>.90$					
Crimes Against Property					
Race					
White	30.4	37.2	32.5	224	100.0
Negro	26.3	32.8	40.9	110	100.0
$x^2 = 2.2$; df $= 2$; P $>.30$					
Occupation					
White collar and skilled	15.0	25.0	60.0	20	100.0
Semi-skilled and unskilled	29.1	33.7	37.2	148	100.0
Unemployed	30.3	41.0	28.7	122	100.0
$x^2 = 8.3$; df $= 4$; P .05					
All Other Crimes					
Race					
White	22.1	34.3	43.6	235	100.0
Negro	28.8	28.8	42.3	184	100.0
$x^2 = 2.5$; df $= 2$; P $>.20$					
Occupation					
White collar and skilled	18.2	24.2	57.6	33	100.0
Semi-skilled and unskilled	14.4	44.9	40.7	270	100.0
Unemployed	25.7	31.5	42.8	70	100.0
$x^2 = 3.4$; df $= 4$; P $>.30$					

larger percentage of whites waits longer than 2 months. The interaction between race and the type of the offense in relation to the length of the delay suggests that the gravity of the offense rather than race prejudice underlies the observed racial difference in the length of delay within a specific offense category; the more serious the crime, the longer the delay. The rather pronounced racial difference in delay in cases of personal crimes—murder, rape, robbery, and aggravated assault—results from a racial difference in patterns of violent crime. Official police records in Ypsilanti reveal a much higher recorded incidence of violent crimes for Negroes (Green, 1970); also Negroes are tried for more serious crimes against the person than whites. Hence the longer delay on the average for Negro defendants reflects the necessity for greater care and more time in the preparation of cases.[3]

The effect on delay of socioeconomic status as measured by work status—whether employed or unemployed and occupational level—is less clear. Although the differences between work categories does not achieve statistical significance, there is some indication that defendants in the upper occupational category enjoy a slight advantage. Table 12.2 shows for cases of personal offenses that there is very little difference between the employed (preponderantly the semi-skilled and unskilled since very few high status persons commit crimes of violence) and the unemployed in the proportions of cases disposed of in less than a month, one to 2 months, and more than 2 months. In cases of property crimes, defendants in the white collar and skilled category take considerably more time to clear the docket than either the semi-skilled and unskilled or the unemployed. Proportionately half as many of the former (15%) compared with the latter two categories (29.1% and 30.3%) take fewer than 31 days and twice as many take longer than two months, 60% to 37.2% and 28.7%, respectively. The findings suggest that persons in the upper occupational levels, who are more financially able and are threatened by a greater loss in status if convicted of theft than persons in the lower working class, invest more in a thorough preparation of their defense. A similar status differential appears in the category of other crimes. The cases of the unemployed are adjudicated in a somewhat larger proportion within the first month after arrest, 25.7%, than the cases of either the semi-skilled and unskilled, 14.4%, or the cases of the white collar and skilled, 18.2%. By the beginning of the third month after arrest, a larger proportion of the cases of those in the higher-status occupation remain unadjudicated compared with those in the lower-status occupation and the unemployed, 57.6% to 40.7% and 42.8%, respectively.

Turning to the municipal court cases (see Table 12.3), again the racial difference is most noticeable, though not statistically significant, in crimes against the person; 76.1% of white cases but

TABLE 12.3

Percentage Distribution of Categories of Number of
Days Elapsed between Arrest and Disposition in
the Municipal Court by Race, and Type of Offense

	0-7 Days	8-30 Days	31 Days and Over	Total N	Pct.
Crimes Against the Person					
Race					
White	76.1	13.4	10.5	67	100.0
Negro	62.9	29.0	8.1	62	100.0
$X^2 = 4.75$; df $= 2$; P $>.05$					
Occupation					
White collar and skilled	54.5	27.3	18.2	11	100.0
Semi-skilled and unskilled	69.3	20.5	10.2	88	100.0
Unemployed	73.3	26.7	0.0	15	100.0
$X^2 = 2.92$; df $= 4$; P $>.50$					
Crimes Against Property					
Race					
White	84.4	7.3	8.3	96	100.0
Negro	78.3	10.9	10.8	46	100.0
$X^2 = .83$; df $= 2$; P $>.50$					
Occupation					
White collar and skilled	63.6	18.2	18.2	11	100.0
Semi-skilled and unskilled	82.8	7.8	9.4	64	100.0
Unemployed	79.3	10.3	10.4	29	100.0
$X^2 = 2.0$; df $= 4$; P $>.70$					
All Other Crimes					
Race					
White	87.8	6.7	5.5	1851	100.0
Negro	87.7	8.3	4.0	751	100.0
$X^2 = 4.1$; df $= 2$; P $>.10$					
Occupation					
White collar and skilled	87.9	6.3	5.8	224	100.0
Semi-skilled and unskilled	87.8	6.9	5.3	1735	100.0
Unemployed	89.1	7.7	3.2	311	100.0
$X^2 = 3.02$; df $= 4$; P $>.50$					

only 62.9% of Negro cases are disposed of within a week. By the end of a month after arrest, the difference is small; 10.5% of white cases and 8.1% of Negro cases await final action. For all other offenses the difference in the length of the period between arrest and conviction is insignificant.

Likewise, among different occupational levels, the differences are generally slight. The longest delay occurs in crimes against the person. A greater percentage of the cases of the unemployed are disposed of within the first week after arrest than those of the unskilled and semi-skilled or the white collar and skilled (73.3 : 69.3 : 54.5). The remainder of the cases of the unemployed are completed by the end of the first month after arrest, whereas 11.1% of the cases of the white collar and skilled and semi-skilled, combined, carry over into the second month. With respect to property offenses, within a week after arrest 79.3% of the cases of the unemployed, 82.8% of the cases of the semi-skilled and unskilled, and 63.6% of the cases of the white collar and skilled clear the docket. One month after arrest the unemployed fall short of the white collar and skilled in the percentage of cases pending, 10.4 to 18.2, but in turn slightly exceed the semi-skilled and unskilled, with only 9.4% of their cases awaiting disposition. For the remainder of offenses the occupational differences are slight although there continues to be a very slight tendency for the cases of the upper status defendants to span a longer period of time between arrest and sentence.

Summary

A study of criminal cases originating in arrests in a small industrial city in the United States reveals a wide variation in the amount of time it takes between arrest and disposition. Delay may be advantageous or disadvantageous to the prosecution or the defense, depending upon the special circumstances of the case. The length of time it takes to process cases appears to be more closely linked to the gravity of the offense than to the social level of the defendant. The lower trial court disposed of more than 80% of its cases within a week after arrest. The higher trial court, understandably, in view of the greater potential loss to the defendant in the event of conviction, operated less quickly. About 55% of its cases were adjudicated by the end of the first month after arrest. Within each court, crimes against the person generally take a longer period to clear the docket than other forms of offenses. The racial and occupational differences in the length of time it takes to process cases is statistically not significant. There is, however, a tendency in the municipal court for the defendant of higher work status to reap whatever advantage, even if only slight, delay may afford in preparing a stout defense. In the circuit court cases, the differences in the average amount of time it takes to process cases by race or socioeconomic status are virtually nil. Since conviction in the circuit court involves potentially a much greater sanction or loss of status than conviction in the municipal court, adequate legal assistance is more apt to be provided to the indigent defendant, which reduces the likelihood that he will suffer any disadvantage from justice delayed.

Notes

1. For a more complete description of the social structural characteristics of Ypsilanti, see Green (1970).
2. Municipal courts have been converted into District Courts under a statewide trial court reorganization plan which became effective in 1970.
3. Psychiatric examinations, the administration and analysis of which consume considerable time and prolong cases, are more likely to be requested for defendants accused of crimes against persons than property crimes.

References

Barrett, Edward S., Jr.
  1965   Criminal justice: The problems of mass production. In
          Harry W. Jones (ed.), The Courts, the Public, and the Law
          Explosion. Englewood Cliffs, N.J.: Prentice-Hall.

Green Edward
  1970   Race, social status, and criminal arrest. American
          Sociological Review, 35: 476-90.

Nagel, Stuart S.
  1965   Disparities in criminal procedure. Paper presented at
          American Sociological Association.

Rosenberg, Maurice
  1965   Court congestion: Status, causes, and proposed remedies.
          In Harry W. Jones (ed.), The Courts, the Public, and the
          Law Explosion. Englewood Cliffs, N.J.: Prentice-Hall.

Sykes, Gresham M.
  1969   Cases, courts, and congestion. In Laura Nader (ed.), Law
          and Culture in Society. Chicago: Aldine.

Zeisel, Hans, Harry Kalven, Jr., and Bernard Buchholz
1959   Delay in the Court. Boston: Little, Brown.

13

REHABILITATION AND
THE JUVENILE COURT:
ARE WE KIDDING OURSELVES?
Sue Titus Reid

So many articles have been written on the juvenile court that it is perhaps presumptuous to write another one. Writers have analyzed the philosophy of the juvenile court, the implementation of that philosophy, and more recently, focused on procedural aspects of the court. It appears that what is still needed, however, is an analysis of the rehabilitative purpose of the court in the light of the possibilities of implementing that purpose.

The juvenile court rests on the basic philosophy that juveniles can be rehabilitated and that, in order to accomplish that goal, they must receive "special handling" which is not provided by the criminal court system. It will be the purpose of this paper to examine that philosophy in the light of available knowledge. Specifically, what empirical evidence is there to support any or all of the claims of the juvenile court?

The early treatment of juveniles in the United States may be traced back to English common law which provided that a child under seven was incapable of committing a crime; a child of seven to 14 years was presumed incapable but that was a rebuttable presumption, and a child over 14 was treated as an adult. Thus, at the age of seven a child could be "guilty" of a felony and punished as an adult. Some children were hanged for their offenses and those who escaped the death penalty often faced corporal punishment and deprivation. With the growing dissatisfaction with this treatment of juveniles, coupled with a general spirit of humanitarianism, reformers succeeded in their advocacy of a system which would emphasize treatment rather than punishment of juveniles. Thus, the juvenile court emerged in 1899 in Illinois.

Philosophy of the Juvenile Court

As the juvenile court was established, jurisdiction could be obtained through the English doctrine of parens patriae, which in the United States was extended to include delinquent as well as dependent and neglected children. The state was considered the "ultimate parent of the child" (Lou, 1927:5), and the proceeding of the juvenile court was to be one by which the state protected the best interests of the child. It was not to be a court of law in the sense of a criminal court. The child was to be protected from the stigma of the criminal court. Rather than a warrant for his arrest, the child would be brought into court by means of a summons; he would not be indicted, but a petition would be filed on his behalf. If detention were necessary, he would be detained in facilities separate from adults but not in jail. He would not have a trial but a hearing which would be private, juries would not be required, and attorneys would rarely, if ever, appear. The hearings would be informal, for the "ordinary trappings" of the courtroom were thought to be out of place in such hearings. The judge would not sentence the child as a form of punishment, but rather would make a disposition of the case, based on the results of a thorough social study undertaken to assist his determination of the treatment method which would be in the best interest of the particular child before the court. Procedural safeguards were not important; in fact, they might hinder rehabilitation of the child. Since the juvenile court acts as the child's parent under the doctrine of parens patriae, solely for the benefit of the child, "it is natural that some of the safeguards of judicial contests should be laid aside" (Van Waters, 1925:163-64).

A new concept of "justice" thus emerged in the juvenile court. Apparently the founders of the juvenile court believed that they were giving the juvenile more protection than he would receive in the criminal court. The juvenile court would go "beyond justice," looking to the total situation, and based upon the findings of behavioral scientists, plan a method of treatment which would grasp the child from a potential criminal career. No longer would the lawbreaker be treated with hostility, prejudice and revenge, but justice would be administered "in the name of truth, love, and understanding" (Lou, 1927:2, note 9).

The emphasis of the juvenile court was clearly on the welfare of the child, with rehabilitation as the primary goal. This "rehabilitative ideal" was based on the assumption that human behavior is the result of antecedent causes and that these causes may be discovered through scientific means (Allen, 1959:226). Individualized treatment for the juvenile offender became a possibility when

society . . . came to realize that justice for children is
not symbolized by a blindfolded goddess dealing out the

same punishment for the same offense, regardless of cause or need, but is symbolized by a goddess with blindfold removed, with a microscope and test tube in her hands, so as to see and understand the total situation and work out a plan that will correct and rehabilitate the child (Nicholas, 1961:159).

Imposition of this rehabilitative ideal (which is also embodied in probation and parole) upon the system of criminal justice created some problems which led Allen (1959:227) to conclude, "I know of no area in which a more effective demonstration can be made of the necessity for greater mutual understanding between the law and the behavioral disciplines." The philosophy of the juvenile court could not be implemented without the scientific knowledge expected from the behavioral sciences.

The Reality of the Juvenile Court

The aim of the interrelationship of law and the behavioral sciences, working through the juvenile court system to rehabilitate juveniles, was a great ideal. But the reality of the system, as indicated by numerous studies, is that the dream of the reformers has not been realized in the United States. "The rhetoric of the juvenile court movement speaks of assistance, treatment, friendly concern," writes Paulsen, 1967b:240, "the reality reflects the hardness of the criminal process." Or, as Mr. Justice Fortas said, "There may be grounds for concern that the child receives the worst of both worlds: that he gets neither the protections accorded to adults nor the solicitous care and regenerative treatment postulated for children."[1]
The reality is that the juvenile court system has failed to remove the "stigma" society attaches to those who violate its criminal laws. The label "juvenile delinquent" may and usually does destroy a child's reputation in his home community and the stigma usually follows him for his entire life. The reality is that the court often deprives the child of his freedom for the commission of acts which, if committed by an adult, would not be unlawful, as illustrated by the case of Gault.[2] In that case, Mr. Justice Fortas, writing the opinion of the Court, said, "Juvenile court history has again demonstrated that unbridled discretion, however benevolently motivated, is frequently a poor substitute for principle and procedure."[3]
The reality is that unlike the founders promised, the juvenile is often detained in jails or lockups. He has in some states been sentenced or administratively transferred to adult institutions by the juvenile court, acting without procedural safeguards. Records of juvenile

hearings have not always been kept private as promised, and juveniles have been adjudicated delinquent on the basis of inaccurate "facts." Thus, what was designed to be a court which would always act in the best interests of the child, providing him with "more than justice," has become an institution which is often arbitrary and unfair.[4]

Another reality of the juvenile court is its failure to prevent delinquency or to rehabilitate those adjudicated delinquent. Realizing the problems involved in interpreting statistics on delinquency, one might argue that the juvenile court does prevent delinquency in that the rates might be much higher today absent the juvenile court. But that is unlikely. On the contrary, it has been argued that the juvenile court has a negative impact on children which in some cases results in leading them into further delinquency (Paulsen, 1967a:72). "It professes to rehabilitate the offender, but the juvenile court often creates abuses worse than those it seeks to correct" (Knudten, 1968:302). Estimates are that roughly half of the juveniles who are placed in institutions by the juvenile court are recidivists (Wheeler and Inskeep, 1968:25). These figures had led some to conclude that the "correctional system is a band-aid operation. It is neither preventive nor curative" (Ibid.: 22).

The most serious problem, however, is that the juvenile court philosophy of treatment, not punishment, has not been realized. In this area, "the dream and the reality have been far apart" (Reed, 1968:642). Institutions which were designed to treat rather than to punish are often more preoccupied with custodial care than with actual treatment. "Experience has demonstrated that, in practice, there is a strong tendency for the rehabilitative ideal to serve purposes that are essentially incapacitative rather than therapeutic in character" (Allen, 1959:229).

A basic explanation for the failure of the juvenile court to live up to its promise to treat, rather than to punish, is that resources are inadequate. The public, at first enthusiastic about establishing the special court for children, has declined to spend sufficient funds to make possible the implementation of the philosophy. Facilities for juveniles are crowded; many do not have probation services; treatment personnel are scarce and often inadequately trained, with the result that custodial problems take precedence over treatment. Juvenile court judges are often untrained and must perform their duties without sufficient probation and social service personnel, and with limited or nonexistent psychological and psychiatric services. Treatment is impossible because of the lack of facilities. Because of the lack of probation and other treatment services, juveniles who could be helped on an out-patient basis are often incarcerated. The literature abounds with examples of types of punishment within the juvenile institutions which would indicate that some juveniles may indeed have "the worst of both worlds."

The problem is more complicated than lack of money, however. The President's Commission (1967:80) noted that a more fundamental problem is the lack of knowledge of treatment and prevention as well as the inability to predict delinquency.

But it is by no means true that a simple infusion of resources into juvenile courts and attendant institutions
would fulfill the expectations that accompanied the court's
birth and development . . .. The failure of the juvenile
court to fulfill its rehabilitative and preventive promise
stems in important measure from a grossly over-optimistic
view of what is known about the phenomenon of juvenile
criminality and of what even a fully equipped juvenile court
could do about it. Experts in the field agree that it is extremely difficult to develop successful methods for pre-
venting serious delinquent acts through rehabilitative programs for the child.

In an analysis of the effect of the Gault decision upon the juvenile court philosophy, Cohen (1968:617) noted that we do not yet have the scientific information necessary for accurate prediction, prevention, control, and treatment of delinquency. He concluded:

If all our courts and correction agencies were staffed by
Ph.D.'s in clinical psychology and sociology and provided
with unlimited resources, we would still not know in many
cases . . . whether the needs of "treatment" would be
better served by letting the offender go free or by incar-
cerating him.

Lack of knowledge is thus the second explanation for the failure of the juvenile court to live up to its promise to treat rather than to punish. One must therefore consider the question of whether the founders created an impossible task with their expectations for the juvenile court. Is there enough empirical evidence to support and to implement the philosophy of the juvenile court to a degree that justifies its continuance?

Empirical Data and the Juvenile
Court Philosophy

It was believed that the juvenile court would avoid the negative effects of the stigma attached to the label of "criminal." However, the "juvenile delinquent" label may also have negative effects. The literature on "labeling theory" supports this allegation. Wheeler and Cottrell (1966:22), in summarizing this literature, state, "The evidence suggests that official response to the behavior in question may initiate processes that push the misbehaving juveniles toward further delinquent conduct, and, at least, make it more difficult for them to re-enter the conventional world." They further point out that this hypothesis "is based upon the concept of labeling and a theory of its consequences." It is not a "finding" supported by substantial empirical evidence. The President's Commission (1967:80), also without systematic empirical evidence, concluded that the labeling process may lead to a self-fulfilling prophecy situation. As a result, "The most informed and benign official treatment of the child therefore contains within it the seeds of its own frustration and itself may often feed the very disorder it is designed to cure."

The fact remains, however, that our understanding of labeling remains mainly theoretical. Certainly there is no substantial empirical evidence which indicates that the harmful effects of labeling have been removed by substituting "delinquent" for "criminal."

Another dimension of the juvenile court philosophy, concerned with the impact of the court procedure on juveniles, is the concept that informality of judges and informality of procedure is preferable to the formality of the adult criminal court. The belief that this in-formality is conducive to rehabilitation of the offender, however, has never been substantiated by empirical evidence. The experts today argue, to the contrary, that the absence of the formality of due process may have a negative effect on the juvenile. The Supreme Court in the Gault decision accepted this theory, as Mr. Justice Fortas stated, "The essentials of due process may be a more impressive and more therapeutic attitude so far as the juvenile is concerned." [5] The Court cited Wheeler and Cottrell who stated that "unless appropriate due process of law is followed, even the juvenile who has violated the law may not feel that he is being fairly treated and may therefore resist the rehabilitative efforts of court personnel." [6] The President's Commission (1967:86) arrived at the same conclusion, stating that "informality has no necessary connection with therapy."

Intertwined with the discussion of formal versus informal pro-cedures is the effect of counsel on the juvenile. It had been feared that the presence of counsel would ruin the therapeutic possibilities of the court. It is too early to know the actual effect of the presence of counsel in juvenile cases, since research in this area has only recently begun on a very large scale. One study, however, conducted in California, which has provided counsel in juvenile cases since 1961, revealed the following:

> Attorneys do their clients some good. A comparison of cases with and without attorneys showed that the former

had a higher percentage of dismissals, fewer wardships declared, and more sentences to the California Youth Authority suspended . . . but . . . the main conclusion reached was that the major contribution of attorneys in the juvenile court lay in their ability to mitigate the severity of dispositions rather than disproving allegations of the petitions (Lemert, 1970:160).

Lemert (1970:161) recognized the potential problem which might exist when the juvenile denies the allegation. If the hearing turned into an adversary one and the probation officer had to play the role of prosecutor, his effectiveness in later working with the juvenile and his parents might be hindered. Lemert concluded, however, that the lawyer in juvenile proceedings is more of a negotiator than an adversary and that his function as the latter is likely to "be marginal." Additional studies will be needed before conclusions can be drawn, but at least it is clear that present evidence does not support the original philosophy of the juvenile court that informal procedures and absence of counsel are prerequisite to rehabilitation. Nor is there evidence that the Supreme Court decisions, which have injected some of the procedural safeguards of the criminal court into juvenile court proceedings, will aid rehabilitation of juveniles. But it might be well to consider the words of Allen (1959:230): "Ignorance, in itself, is not disgraceful so long as it is unavoidable. But when we rush to measures affecting human liberty and human dignity on the assumption that we know what we do not know or can do what we cannot do, then the problem of ignorance takes on a more sinister hue."
But what about the basic philosophy of the juvenile court—that the juvenile can be rehabilitated through treatment programs? The crucial question is whether enough is known about treatment to justify a special court for juveniles.
In analyzing the current knowledge about treatment of juveniles, it must first be recognized that the lack of sophisticated empirical research is not a result of disinterest or inactivity on the part of social scientists, but rather methodological problems which make such research difficult and, in some cases, impossible. The literature on juvenile delinquency is extensive, but much of the "evidence" is theoretical, speculative, impressionistic opinions which have yet to be substantiated by careful, systematic, empirical research. Most studies of the etiology of delinquency are based on surveys which are noted for their sampling problems. Samples are often drawn from institutionalized populations and therefore are not representative of all juvenile crime. Often they do not utilize control groups. In addition, researchers cannot agree on the definition of juvenile delinquency, and the measurement of delinquency is further complicated by the

fact that the definitions differ from jurisdiction to jurisdiction, often within the same state. Even if researchers could agree on a legal definition of those acts which constitute a delinquency offense, they would still face a problem in defining delinquent persons. Several studies have indicated that most young people commit at least one act for which they could be adjudicated delinquent; yet most of these young people are not labeled juvenile delinquent. Additional problems in studying delinquency result from the lack of tools for measuring critical variables. Methodological problems thus seriously limit research potential in the area of the causes of juvenile delinquency.

Treatment programs may involve mainly sociological approaches to the treatment of juveniles; or may be primarily psychological or psychiatric in their orientation, or a combination of all of these approaches. They may or may not be oriented toward the total community or the juvenile. Furthermore, it is difficult to generalize because most of the programs are experimental and involve small samples. Often they are limited to certain types of delinquents. They are difficult to evaluate. Nevertheless, a glance at some of these programs may reveal enough progress in the treatment of juveniles to justify the continuation of the specialized system of reaction to the juvenile offender.

Sociologists have emphasized the importance of the social structure in understanding delinquency and crime. Durkheim, the first to argue that crime is normal and functional, laid the foundation for later theories regarding the importance of social structure. Merton, in developing the theory of anomie, clearly rejected individualistic explanations of behavior, and attempted to understand behavior in terms of the social structure within which that behavior occurs. Social structures exert pressure on some persons to conform and on others to deviate. Sutherland, like Merton and Durkheim, tried to explain delinquent behavior within the context of the person's environment. His theory of differential association is essentially a learning theory which states that criminal and delinquent behavior is learned in small intimate groups. Attempts to change that behavior must concentrate on the group as well as on the individual (Cressey, 1966). The subculture theories of Cohen, Miller, and Cloward and Ohlin also emphasize the influence which groups have upon juvenile behavior. The emphasis on the delinquent's environment has thus been central in the work of sociologists who have attempted to understand delinquent behavior.

Beginning with one of the early treatment programs (the Chicago Area Project), sociologists have argued that unless the environment of the child can be changed, treatment will be ineffective. The Project followed the extensive studies of delinquency conducted in Chicago by Shaw and McKay (1942). Although criticized because of the deterministic conclusions of the researchers, the studies are significant because of the importance imputed to the environment in explaining delinquent behavior. The Project was designed to activate positive changes in the environment of the slums. Shaw based his plan on the theory which emphasized the importance of primary group relationships in determining which social values are important to an individual, and on ecological theories which emphasize the impact of the total environment. He concluded that the Project would be a failure unless the desire for a treatment-prevention program came from within and was administered from within the community. Kobrin (1964), in assessing the success of the program 25 years after its inception, noted the difficulty in evaluating such programs, but he believed that it had reduced delinquency. Kobrin underscored the need to enlist the power of discipline in primary groups in order to enhance the effectiveness of correctional agencies. He noted that most treatment programs result in serious loss of control of the conduct of the young person because he is treated as one of a category, not as an individual human being. The delinquent must not be neglected, despised or ignored as a person but rather, dealt with as a person worthy of consideration. Treatment programs must deal directly with the delinquent and with his total environment.

One of the most famous treatment facilities was initiated in New Jersey in 1950 and became known as the Highfields Project (McCorkle, Elias, and Bixby, 1958; Weeks, 1970). The Project was designed as an alternative to incarceration and probation. It was thought that short-term treatment might be effective for some juveniles. The Project was limited to males, ages 16-17, who were assigned directly from the court, and did not include recidivists or mentally disturbed boys. The goal was to rehabilitate these delinquents within three to four months. They were housed in an old mansion and were to live as normally as possible. The program involved no formal education, but the boys did work. They read papers, listened to radio, and had hobby and craft activities. The only formal treatment consisted of group counseling sessions. The success of the program has been a matter of debate, but it appears that it is as least as successful as a reformatory, and probably more so. Clearly, it is less expensive and involves much less time than the ordinary institutional program.

Variations on the Highfields Project are seen in programs developed at Essenfield, New Jersey and the Pinehills experiment in Provo, Utah. In both of these programs, the delinquent continues to live at home. Unlike Highfields, habitual offenders were placed in the Provo Experiment, although highly disturbed and psychotic boys were not included. Like Highfields, the groups were small (limited to 20). Peer group interaction was stressed. The first phase of the program involved intensive group work, and the second phase centered on helping the boy after release. This involved attempting to maintain reference group support for the boy and community action to help him find employment. The Provo experiment included a design for measuring the effectiveness of the program, and the indications are that the experiment was more successful than the program of the state school (Empey and Rabow, 1961).

Another program which has shown some success in the rehabilitation of "high-risk" delinquents is the Annex of Boys' Training Schools in New York City, which began in 1947. The program includes psychological and psychiatric services, weekly therapy or counseling sessions, off-campus activities, and provides the boys with opportunities for self-achievement and self-discipline. The philosophy is that treatment is more than management. "Treatment is help; it is the opportunity for social and emotional growth" (Kane, 1966:41). The emphasis is upon the therapeutic milieu, with the total living situation considered to be the milieu. When the boys receive a release date, they are immediately placed in a pre-release therapy group to help prepare for the transition from institution to family life. In an analysis of the program, the director of the institution suggested that the same kind of intensive services needs to be applied to the family of the delinquent and to the after-care of the boy once he is released. In evaluating the Annex, the director indicated that the success of treating high-risk delinquents can be attributed to the small size of the institution (100), with a large staff (99 full-time and 10 part-time), the intensive visual supervision, and the totality of treatment effort.

Emphasis on individualized treatment is the key philosophy of the National Training School for Boys, also called the Robert F. Kennedy Youth Center, at Morgantown, West Virginia. The ten million dollar institution, opened in 1969, houses around 300 federal offenders, ages 16 to 20, and employs a staff of 170 full-time persons. "The program on which each new student embarks is individualized and flexible to meet his changing needs. . . . Every possible area of institutional life is integrated and directed toward the treatment objective" (Gerard, 1970:38).

These treatment programs are cited to illustrate that they have experienced some success in rehabilitating delinquents. The list is not meant to be inclusive, but only to illustrate modern programs for treatment of juveniles, programs which would probably be hindered if not eliminated if the flexibility for handling juveniles, characteristic of the juvenile court were abolished. Their success should indicate that enough progress in the treatment of juveniles has been made to continue the juvenile court, with its stress upon treatment rather than punishment. With an emphasis upon the dignity of the juvenile and an attempt to create a positive atmosphere for rehabilitation, these programs perhaps lend support to two hypotheses which should be considered in an analysis of treatment efforts.

The first hypothesis is that a juvenile cannot be treated adequately if he is hostile toward the system, as he may be if he views the system as unjust. Judge Paulsen (1964:9) has pointed out that the average juvenile who comes before the juvenile court for adjudication does not have the faith and trust in the system necessary for treatment. Paulsen suggests that because of this basic lack of trust which the juvenile has for the system, treatment may be impossible. "A young-ster who has experienced an unfair proceeding is an impossible sub-ject for rehabilitation," writes Paulsen. A second hypothesis is that the juvenile cannot be rehabilitated in an authoritarian setting. Some of the programs discussed above specifically emphasize the importance of allowing the juvenile some freedom to make decisions and discipline himself within the treatment program.

The conclusion may be that the juvenile court philosophy is not inherently incompatible with rehabilitation of delinquents, but that it has been hindered in its attempts to treat and to rehabilitate by other elements of the philosophy—namely, the informality which resulted in a lack of procedural safeguards and which created a system that in many cases gave the juvenile the "worst of both worlds." It seems clear that the lack of procedure did not aid rehabilitation, and it there-fore seems wise to suggest that before the juvenile court is abolished, one should carefully study the effects of relevant Supreme Court deci-sions on the court. Perhaps by injecting procedural safeguards into the juvenile court, the treatment philosphy will become more of a reality. This might be accomplished by dividing the juvenile court into two stages: adjudication and disposition. The first would involve all of the elements of procedural due process, while the second would embody the original juvenile court philosophy of individualized treat-ment. In 1968, the National Conference of Commissioners on Uniform State Laws proposed such a division. Under this proposal, the first stage, adjudication, would include all of the elements of procedural due process, with a requirement of proof beyond a reasonable doubt. The second stage, disposition, would require only evidence which is clear and convincing. Of those juveniles adjudicated delinquent in the first stage, only those deemed in need of treatment would be handled in the second stage. Thus, a juvenile might be adjudicated delinquent and then released (Burdick, 1968:48-49). This proposal would allow the flexibility necessary for individualized treatment, thus preserving the basic philosophy of the juvenile court. The stage of disposition would involve "a special juvenile treatment bureau at work, inter-disciplinary in composition, with behavioral scientists cooperating with social scientists to solve a human and social problem—juvenile delinquency"(Milton, 1970:91). As for the lack of knowledge about treatment, social scientists do have some understanding of juvenile delinquency, and "as long as we pursue the rehabilitative ideal, then it is to that wisdom, no matter how imperfect, that we must turn" (Croxton, 1967:11).

Bifurcation of the juvenile court, however, will not alone solve the problem. The necessary money for treatment facilities and personnel is needed. The legal profession must provide well-trained juvenile court judges. Society will have to make a commitment to accept the juvenile who returns to society from a state institution; a commitment to offer him all the help and encouragement which he needs for rehabilitation rather than dismiss him quickly because of the "stigma of delinquency." If the total environment of the child is involved in his delinquency, the total environment must be involved in his treatment program. Without this support, the juvenile court is doomed to failure. But there is hope for success.

> With fresh knowledge we think we can convince the public critics and the legal scholars that the juvenile court system can be made to work effectively and that it can assure equal justice for all juveniles. . . . Where the public and the professions combine forces, the hopes of its founders may be fulfilled (Ketcham, 1966:288).

Notes

1. Kent v. United States, 383 U.S. 541 (1966).
2. In re Gault, 387 U.S. 1 (1967).
3. Ibid., p. 18.
4. Ibid., pp. 18-20.
5. Ibid. p. 26.
6. Ibid. p. 26.

References

Allen, F.
  1959 Criminal justice, legal values and the rehabilitative ideal. Journal of Criminal Law, Criminology and Police Science, 50: 226-32.

Burdick, E.
  1968 The Uniform Juvenile Court Act. Pennsylvania Bar Association Quarterly, 40(October): 47-56.

Cohen, A.
  1968 An evaluation of Gault by a sociologist. Indiana Law Journal, 43: 614-18.

Cressey, D.
1966   Changing criminals: The application of the theory of dif-
        ferential association. In R. Giallombardo (ed.), Juvenile
        Delinquency: A Book of Readings. New York: Wiley.

Croxton, T. A.
1967   Kent case and its consequence. Journal of Family Living,
        7(Spring): 1-13.

Empey, L., and J. Rabow
1961   The Provo experiment in delinquency rehabilitation. Ameri-
        can Sociological Review, 26: 679-96.

Gerard, R.
1970   Institutional innovations in juvenile corrections. Federal
        Probation, 34(December): 37-44.

Kane, J.
1966   An institutional program for the seriously disturbed delin-
        quent boy. Federal Probation, 30(September): 37-44.

Ketcham, O. W.
1966   Juvenile court for 1975. Social Service Review, 40: 283-88.

Knudten, R. (Ed.).
1968   Criminological Controversies. New York: Appleton-Century-
        Crofts.

Kobrin, S.
1964   The Chicago Area Project. In R. Cavan (ed), Readings in
        Juvenile Delinquency. Philadelphia: Lippincott.

Lemert, E.
1970   The juvenile court: Quest and realities. In P. Garabedian
        and D. Gibbons (eds.). Becoming Delinquent: Young Of-
        fenders and the Correctional System. Chicago: Aldine.

Lou, H.
1927   Juvenile Courts in the United States. Chapel Hill, N.C.:
        University of North Carolina Press.

McCorkle, L., A. Elias, and F. Bixby
1958   The Highfields Story. New York: Henry Holt.

Milton, M.
  1970   Post-Gault: A new prospectus for the juvenile court. New
          York Law Forum 16: 57-92.

Nicholas, F. W.
  1961   History, philosophy, and procedures of juvenile courts.
          Journal of Family Law, 1: 151-71.

Paulsen, M. G.
  1964   Do children have rights? PTA Magazine, 58(February):
          7-9.
  1967a   Role of juvenile courts. Current History, 53(August): 70-75.
  1967b   The constitutional domestication of the juvenile court. Su-
          preme Court Review, 233-66.

President's Commission on Law Enforcement and Adminsitration of
Justice

  1967   The Challenge of Crime in a Free Society. Washington:
          Government Printing Office.

Reed, A.
  1968   Gault and the juvenile training school. Indiana Law Journal
          43: 641-54.

Shaw, C., and H. McKay
  1942   Juvenile Delinquency and Urban Areas. Chicago: University
          of Chicago Press.

Van Waters, M.
  1925   Youth in Conflict. New York: Republic Publishing.

Weeks, H.
  1970   The Highfields Project and its success. In N. Johnston et al.
          (eds.), The Sociology of Punishment and Correction. 2nd
          ed., New York: Wiley.

Wheeler, G., and H. Inskeep III
  1968   Youth in the gaunlet. Federal Probation, 32(December):
          21-25.

Wheeler, S., and L. Cottrell, Jr. (with assistance of A. Romasco)
  1966   Juvenile Delinquency: Its Prevention and Control. New
          York: Russell Sage Foundation.

14

**THE SYSTEMATIC AND
THE COMPOSITE MODELS
FOR PLANNING AND
EVALUATION OF THE
CRIMINAL JUSTICE SYSTEM**
Peter P. Lejins

The Systemic and the Composite Models

The focal proposition of this paper is that in the planning and the corresponding evaluation of crime control measures, all of the major methods of such control—punitive sanctions, cause removing, and the mechanical protection of society—must constantly be considered together, rather than pursuing this control in terms of only one of these methods without regard for the effect which this has on the other two. This writer proposes to refer to this approach as the systemic planning and evaluation model, which means that the planning must be done in terms of the total system of criminal justice rather than in terms of only one of the above-mentioned methods. The reason for the importance of such emphasis is the fact that in reality usually the opposite is true. Moreover, in addition to the systemic model, a composite planning model is suggested, which, besides what is implied in the systemic model, includes in the planning of crime control measures consideration of the cultural setting within the given society, the resources available for crime control with cost benefit analysis as one of the major planning and evaluation tools, and the standards of quality controls accepted in the given society with regard to social action programs (Lejins, 1971).

The systemic point of view is, of course, applicable regardless of which of the three crime control methods is being planned for, but at the present juncture of historical developments in criminal justice, the systemic point of view should be introduced and emphasized, especially with regard to planning in corrections, that is, the cause-removing or behavior modification of the criminal offenders. Here is the historical perspective within which this statement is being made.

Historical Perspective

Although all three methods of crime control—punishment, correction and incapacitation—could probably be found in all human societies in varying proportions at all times, it is quite obvious that up to the end of the 18th century, in Western society, punishment and incapacitation were by far the prevalent methods of control. Only toward the end of that century did the correctional handling of offenders, meaning programs focused on the removal of the reasons or causes for criminal behavior and thus modifying the offender's behavior from criminal to noncriminal, begin to be emphasized. The major factor in this shift to the correctional approach was the emergence of behavioral and social science in the 19th century, which meant the interpretation of human behavior in terms of "causes," with the resulting propositions that the best way to eliminate the undesirable behavior is to remove its causes or the reasons for it—its motivations, criminogenic factors, or whatever the terminology. From this followed the need to study the etiology of criminal behavior—the discipline of criminology—which was ushered in so dramatically by Lombroso and the positivist school. Criminology, prevention, correction, and the development of correctional, cause-removing or behavior modification methodologies was the sequel.

The suggestion to control crime by cause-removal, as the most logical and effective method, always contained within itself the implication that this method was superior to the punitive method, and hence the advocates of the criminological approach, by the very logic of the situation, were usually skeptical about punishment. Similarly, removal of the causes and behavior modification appear to be superior to the method of protecting society by mechanical measures, i.e. the incapacitation of the offender.

Parenthetically, it should be mentioned that another powerful ideological stream opposed to punitive crime control stemmed from humanitarianism, a social philosophy which swept Western society soon after the advent of the Reformation. Punishment as the deliberate imposition of suffering goes against the grain of humanitarian philosophy. Although correctional and humanitarian considerations are quite different in nature, the one being a completely rational proposition in terms of the ends-means scheme directed toward the removal of criminal behavior by removing the causes, while the other is based on the acceptance of the value premise that suffering is something negative and has to be removed from human society, both clearly create an attitudinal climate unfavorable to punitive crime control (Lejins, 1957, 1970).

Current Controversies and Antagonisms

By now, however, there is another and perhaps even more influential factor in the opposition by corrections-oriented circles to punishment and—to a lesser although still quite significant extent—to incapacitation. This is the complex of gradually developed competitive and antagonistic attitudes on the part of correctional workers and the carriers of the correctional ideology generally toward the punitive programs of crime control and the personnel staffing them. From the early historical beginnings the proposed correctional measures, as substitutes for punitive measures, had been greeted with antagonism not only by the personnel of the old punitive system but also by prevailing public opinion. The latter was accustomed to see crime controlled by punishment and was very hesitant to agree to experimentation in dealings with criminals, an area that has always been a very sensitive one and in which experimentation has been viewed as a risky and dangerous proposition. Thus the advocates of correctional reform found themselves for two centuries in a slow uphill fight, being for a long time regarded as pariahs in the criminal justice field, and only slowly gaining some recognition for their methods. Their need to promote these correctional measures, their firm belief in them, the sense that they were being unfairly handicapped by those in power (who, in the opinion of the correctional advocates, did not fully understand the more sophisticated correctional approach and were probably acting in defense of their vested interests)—all this led to disdain and distrust of the punitive system, both its theory and its practices, on the part of the correctional protagonists. The punitive crime control system was the obstacle in the way of the correctional reformer and thus became the enemy.

There developed a highly important byproduct of this situation. The causal analysis of criminal behavior by the emerging social sciences led to an intensive study of the etiology of criminal behavior and to experimentation with cause-removing methods. On the other hand, "the enemy," the punitive sanctions, were not what the social scientists and especially those in the area of corrections would be interested in studying or would want to "honor" with research. Thus, slowly but surely a situation developed that is characteristic also of the present, with an enormous amount of research with regard to the etiology of crime and corrections, but practically none concerning the effectiveness of the punitive methods.

It is significant that some scholars have recently become engaged in an attempt to revive interest and scientific inquiry into the effects of punishment and especially general deterrence: e.g. the program of studies in the area of deterrence of the Center for Studies in Criminal Justice at the University of Chicago by Norval Morris,

Frank Zimring and their associates (Zimring, 1971). There are a number of individual researchers who have turned their attention to this topic, so that sporadic research reports are beginning to appear.

Thus, in addition to whatever the theoretical and research-proven practical advantages of corrections may be over and above punitive sanctions and incapacitation, one must reckon with the deeply ingrained living ideology of a now powerful professional group that is strongly antipunishment, tries to ignore it, and attempts in practice competitively to push it out and to replace it. This does not constitute a favorable climate for an impartial assessment and evaluation of the effectiveness of punitive sanctions and of the desirability of using them alternatingly and together with correctional measures.

Present Stance of Corrections

As the result of the above-indicated historical development and thus the current situation, in the United States, at least, correctional measures, programs and institutions in the planning and evaluation of their activities are concerned exclusively with the behavior-modification task in terms of eliminating motivations leading to criminal behavior, i.e. making noncriminals out of criminals. Thus corrections has adopted the medical or treatment model. Research consists in a search for criminogenic factors; treatment means procedures used to eliminate these factors; and evaluation depends on the extent to which offenders cease to be offenders and no longer commit crimes. In a sense the correctional crime-control programs ideally approach research in behavior modification, and evaluation of action programs tests hypotheses in the same way that Ph.D. dissertations do. With this methodology at hand, there are many indications that the correctional field is ready and willing to take on the total responsibility for the control of criminal behavior. The performance of the punitive function is given very little attention in any of the correctional programs, if it is mentioned at all. When voices are raised about punishment, the correctional programs involving incarceration provide the convenient general answer that the limitation of freedom by incarceration is the suffering imposed as punishment, and dismiss the issue with that. What the answer of community-based corrections will be to an inquiry about the performance of the punitive function is anybody's guess. Note that in the Working Papers of the National Commission on Reform of Federal Criminal Laws in 1970, the proposal is made to substitute the title "Correctional Code" for the traditional title "Penal Code."

Current Skepticism About Corrections

And yet, there are many clouds on the horizon of correctional euphoria. The data seems to indicate that the behavior of offenders is not being modified by the correctional programs, and that offenders continue to be offenders. The issue is of such recent national prominence in the United States that it is hardly necessary to dwell on it in detail. There is always room for legitimate debate, of course, regarding the true rates of recidivism, and there is always the subterfuge of the difference between the proposed ideal programs and their imperfect implementation, with insufficient funds, poorly trained personnel, and lack of public support being blamed. At their worst, these indices of failure might well be illustrated by the by now famous quotation from former Attorney General Ramsey Clark's book, Crime in America (1970), to the effect that over 80% of the felonies in the United States are committed by persons who have previously been sentenced for felonies and must therefore in most cases have undergone some form of correctional intervention, a fact which testifies to a catastrophic if not total failure of the American correctional system.

A Remedy in the Current Crisis

Perhaps the dilemma or the failure of the contemporary correctional approach lies in the circumstance that corrections refuses to face the fact that in all societies, including contemporary societies and the United States, correction is not the only method of dealing with criminal offenders. There are such other methods as punitive sanctions and incapacitating the offender in order to protect society from him. All three of these methods of dealing with offenders are fully recognized, corrections notwithstanding, and are used in the United States; they permeate the country's legislation—inclusive of the Constitution—and administrative practice at all levels of government; moreover, the general public expects them to be used as well.

There is, then, the question of what the relationship of the correctional method to punitive control and protection of society should be. Unfortunately, in spite of its obvious importance, this question is discussed very little, and the prevailing situation in the U.S. can be characterized as one where the personnel responsible for the implementation of the three functions—the police, the prosecution, the courts and correction—simply act in terms of the traditional historical functions assigned to them and compete with each other for the scopes of authority as any professional group would be expected to do in terms of their respective interests. It can be said that when the point is made, as is frequently done, that the American criminal justice system is not a system but a nonsystem, the meaning of this statement should be taken to be not only that the police, the prosecution, the courts and corrections are working independently of each other, or even at cross purposes, but also, that the performance of their major tasks—punishment, incapacitation and/or correction—is not rationally coordinated. From that standpoint the American criminal justice system is doubly a nonsystem. This is the sense of the recommendation of this paper, that a systemic model of planning and evaluation be used instead of engaging in independent planning and evaluation for each one of the three methods separately. This means that in the process of planning and evaluation, criminal justice measures, whether punitive, incapacitating or correctional, should not be looked upon only as entities in themselves, but also as components of one and the same system which must be planned and evaluated in their mutual interrelationship with one another, assessing not only the effectiveness of each one individually, but also the effect of each on the effectiveness of the other two.

Systemic Evaluation Exemplified

It is rather widely recognized that the major function of the punitive sanctions in the criminal law system is the general deterrence of all potential offenders. Criminal law generally exercises a preventive influence by means of this deterrence, and it is usually granted that the effectiveness of general deterrence in the long run depends on the administration of punishment to the individual offender whenever an offense is committed. The certainty and the celerity of punishment are presumably the key to the success of this system of crime control. Hence, replacement of punitive sanctions by correctional treatment is bound to have an effect on the results of general deterrence. Thus, for instance, a change from mixed punitive-correctional measures, such as incarceration in correctional institutions—where the limitation of freedom performs the punitive function, while correctional programs are supposed to bring about the desired behavior modification—to community-based treatment, which contains very little of punishment, should be evaluated not only in terms of the behavior-modification value of community-based treatment, but also in terms of the effect of this change on the functioning of general deterrence. The same applies with reference to the protection of society by means of incapacitation of the offender. A reasonable amount of the needed incapacitation cannot be sacrificed in favor of correctional experimentation any more than excessive incapacitation should be allowed to stand in the way of correctional treatment. Thus, the evaluation

160

of correctional measures in terms of their theoretical and empirical justification as behavior modifiers must be supplemented by systemic evaluation.

At the current juncture of intensive controversies regarding both the theory and the practical measures in the area of crime control, it is perhaps important to point out that the suggested systemic planning model does not necessarily promote any one of the three basic methods of dealing with crime, i.e. punishment, correction or incapacitation, in preference to the other two. It only suggests that a rational coordination of the three methods is an indispensible necessity. Specifically, it does not suggest a greater emphasis either on the punitive sanctions or on the cause-removing activities. A supporter of one of the three methods, who would claim that the systemic model exudes some partiality, would be acting in terms of the well-known proposition: "Who is not with us is against us." The systemic model suggests that before promoting some correctional measure, one should assay what the use of this measure will do to the performance of the punitive and incapacitating sanctions. If, for instance, this measure, as the total reaction of the society to the convicted offender, means elimination of practically all suffering except for a mild inconvenience, the question should be asked directly and squarely: Are we ready to give up punishment, especially in the sense of general deterrence or general prevention, in the control of crime? If, after serious policy determination on this basic topic of social control, the answer is yes, we are ready to give up punishment, then the systemic model does not necessarily suggest that we could not do so and that we should not use exclusively correctional methods. The systemic model attempts, however, to prevent one category of crime control workers from going ahead with their specific methdology without a rational assessment of what is being done to the other two basic methods and finding out whether the society is willing to accept this effect. If it is not considered wise to accept the consequences, then of course the cause-removing activity is recommended against. This latter determination does not, however, preclude the exploration of that methodology as "pure research," but without any illusions of its being usable at the present time, and perhaps with the main justification that, as an item of knowledge, it could be fed as an element into the decision-making process with regard to the overall strategies of the criminal justice criminal justice crime control system at some future time. Exactly the same position is maintained by the systemic model also with regard to the maintenance, development and promotion of the punitive measures and the incapacitating measures.

Application of the Systemic Model

The systemic approach to the control of criminal behavior could be utilized at four specific points:

1. The three methods used to control criminal behavior—punishment, correction and incapacitation—must be accepted as tasks of the entire criminal justice system. All subsystems must be aware of this fact and each of them must perform certain portions of the above task. At the same time the punitive, correctional or incapacitating measures to be applied in the case of a given offender must be clearly specified by the appropriate authority, probably the court.

Many might assume that the above recommendation is superfluous because it suggests what already exists. Nothing could be further from the truth. As the result of the collision of the old punitive system of crime control with the new correctional treatment plan, without appropriate rational planning as to the quantity and type of punishment, correction or incapacitation, a chaotic situation presently prevails, where the different subsystems of the criminal justice system, or parts thereof, have personnels which are oriented toward one of the three methods only and operate with total oblivion of or even antagonism toward other accepted goals of the system.

It may appear paradoxical, but most people in the United States assume that, as the result of the action of the police and the courts, criminals are brought to punishment; and yet the courts, which prescribe punishment, deliver the offenders to a system which in principle is no longer concerned with punishment, and where punishment remains almost exclusively a byproduct of the correctional programs as a sort of inconvenience imposed on the offender because of the need to have him available for correctional interventions. The average citizen would be very much surprised to learn that, once the offender leaves the court, there is no further punishment-directed effort. The significant thing is that what is left of punishment is a sort of remnant of the old system, and what is being striven for under the label of "progressive" is a purely correctional system, which does not accord any place to punishment.

The once elaborate system of criminal-justice punishments has by now been reduced almost exclusively to fines and incarceration. The only recent discussion of incarceration as punishment has been in terms of limiting the punitive aspects of incarceration exclusively to the limitation of personal freedom, with no other rights lost by the offender. The issue of how effective a punitive measure this constitutes is hardly the topic of any discussion, not to speak of research.

Two observations which are sometimes made may be worth careful pondering. One is that there is effective punishment in this country only in the case of a citizen who has not previously been convicted of crime and who does not belong to those groups that do not assign any meaning to court actions of the "establishment." To that type of person, the stigma attached to being pronounced a criminal offender is real suffering and punishment. It is the only real punishment still in existence. To those who have already committed offenses or belong to the groups that have successfully rationalized away the significance of the punitive action of the state, there is very little deterrence, except some inconvenience caused by temporary incarceration. The second observation referred to is that the only real deterrent quality of modern incarceration is the fear of mistreatment at the hand of other inmates.

2. With regard to each measure or program operated by a criminal justice agency, there has to be an explicit understanding of the objectives to be accomplished and how the realization of these objectives affects the functions of other criminal-justice system agencies and the realization of the three overall objectives. Here reference should be made to the above-cited example of the relationship between the satisfaction of the punitive needs and the correctional needs of community-based treatment.

3. The planning of agencies for the performance of one specific objective should be done in terms of the total system of criminal justice, the specific objective to be achieved, and the niche which the particular agency is to occupy within the total system. An example would be the planning of an institution serving exclusively the purpose of incapacitating certain offenders without any punitive or correctional elements, e.g. preventive detention institutions for "habitual" offenders, as rigorously implemented at one time in England.

4. Another possible application of the systemic model which should be explored is with reference to our present approach to criminal offenders as constituting a homogeneous population in the sense that all are equal before the law and therefore should suffer the same consequences for their crimes. This is not necessarily the most effective way of handling the crime problem. There is a good possibility that the three methods of criminal justice, punishment, protection and correction should be used differentially, depending on the offense and the offender. The final answer will be given by research, but at least as a hypothesis it is a reasonable proposition that some criminal law violators might best respond to punitive measures, others can be handled only by incapacitation, while still others are the proper subjects for correctional treatment. Again, to use an example, it seems quite obvious that such an offense as fraudulent tax returns can be controlled only in terms of general deterrence and therefore calls for punitive sanctions; a youthful offender, on the other hand, who became involved in criminal activities as the result of growing up in a highly delinquent area, would appear

to be a proper subject for correctional intervention. It could well be that the future of an effective rational criminal justice system lies in such differential handling of different types of offenders and offenses.

The Composite Planning Model

With the above characterizations of the systemic model and some of the suggested forms of application, it is proposed here that planning in terms of the systemic model alone is not enough, and one must go beyond the limits of the criminal justice system in planning crime control measures. For this purpose the composite planning and evaluation model is suggested, which has the systemic model as one of its components. Three additional components are suggested:

1. The cultural setting of the given society within which the crime control measures are supposed to be applied must be taken into consideration. The crime-control measures must be compatible with the values and ideals of the given society. Thus, for instance, for the U.S., acceptance from the point of view of the humanitarian principle must be observed, requiring the humane and decent treatment of all, including offenders. Some of the values and ideals pertain to the basics of the social and legal order of the given society, and in the U.S., for instance, are expressed in the Constitution. Thus, any punitive treatment or incapacitating measures in this country must be acceptable from the point of view of their constitutionality.

2. The resources available for crime control in the given society must be considered. By way of an example, a correctional method which requires an inordinate amount of professional time to be spent on an individual offender may be totally impractical, regardless of its potential effectiveness. No society can afford to have as highly trained a correctional agent as a psychiatrist, for instance, working full time to correct no more than ten offenders in one year. American society could not afford 20,000 psychiatrists working full time with 200,000 inmates of state and federal correctional institutions. Cost-benefit analysis is an all-important tool when we are dealing with limited resources, and the resources of any society are necessarily limited in terms of dollars, personnel, time, and training investment in the personnel. Cost-benefit analysis must be applied both within the criminal justice system for the comparative evaluation of correctional, punitive and protective measures, and within the society as a whole as to what resources it can afford to assign to the handling of the crime problem in preference to the satisfaction of other social needs.

3. The standards and quality controls developed in the given society in the operation of its social action programs must be taken

into consideration. The criteria used in the so-called accreditation and licensing of both agencies and professional workers can serve as a good example of what is meant here. Certain standards for the educational background, training and experience of personnel, coupled with manageable case loads, logistic support in terms of a modern and convenient physical plant, office and other machinery, electronic data processing and storage, an effective management information system assuring rapid feedback for rapid decision making, are some of the examples of the criteria which should be observed both in planning and evaluation.

Clarity and Explicitness—A Basic Requirement

In conclusion, the effective utilization of both the systemic and the composite model in the planning and evaluation of crime control measures requires a clear and explicit statement of the goals, objectives and premises of that system, as well as the methods and techniques to be used in all criminal justice programs, so that a rational operation is possible and unjustified traditionalism and faddism—the greatest crippling enemies of the criminal justice system—are eliminated as much as possible.

References

Clark, Ramsey
    1970   Crime in America. New York: Simon and Schuster.

Lejins, Peter P.
    1957   Penal reform and the American Correctional Association. Proceedings of 87th Annual Congress of Correction.
    1970   Ideas which have moved corrections. Proceedings of 100th Annual Congress of Correction.
    1971   Methodologies in the evaluation of correctional programs. Proceedings of the 101st Annual Congress of Correction.

Zimring, Franklin E.
    1971   Perspectives on Deterrence. National Institute of Mental Health, Public Health Service Publication 2056.

Ronald L. Akers, Ph.D., University of Kentucky, 1966; Professor, Department of Criminology, Florida State University.

Roger Baldwin, Ph.D., New York University, 1967; Associate Professor, Muhlenberg College.

Thomas Barker, M.A., Mississippi State University, 1973; N.D.E.A. Fellow and Ph.D. candidate at Mississippi State.

William J. Bowers, Ph.D., Columbia University, 1966; Director, Russell B. Stearns Center for Applied Social Research, Northeastern University.

Bernard Cohen, Ph.D., University of Pennsylvania, 1968; Associate Professor, Queens College of City University of New York.

Wayne L. Cotton, Ph.D., New York University, 1971; Lecturer in Sociology, City College of City University of New York.

Douglas F. Cousineau, Ph.D., University of Alberta, 1974; Lecturer in Sociology, Glendon College of York University.

Edward Green, Ph.D., University of Pennsylvania, 1959; Professor and Head, Department of Sociology, Eastern Michigan University.

Stanley E. Grupp, Ph.D., Indiana University, 1967; Professor, Illinois State University.

Richard L. Henshel, Ph.D., Cornell University, 1969; Associate Professor, University of Western Ontario.

Jerome Himelhoch, Ph.D., Columbia University, 1952; Professor, University of Missouri-St. Louis.

Peter P. Lejins, Ph.D., University of Chicago, 1938; Professor and Director, Institute of Criminal Justice and Criminology, University of Maryland.

Sue Titus Reid, Ph.D., University of Missouri, 1965; J.D., University of Iowa, 1972; Associate Professor and Head, Department of Sociology, Coe College.

Julian Roebuck, Ph.D., University of Maryland; Professor, Mississippi State University.

Edward Sagarin, Ph.D., New York University, 1966; Associate Professor, City College of City University of New York; President, American Society of Criminology, 1973-74.

Clifford D. Shearing, M.A., University of Toronto, 1968; Research Associate and Special Lecturer, Centre of Criminology, University of Toronto.

Emilio C. Viano, Ph.D., New York University, 1973; Associate Professor, The American University.

CORRECTIONS: PROBLEMS OF PUNISHMENT
AND REHABILITATION
                    edited by Edward Sagarin and
                    Donal E. J. MacNamara

CRIME AND DELINQUENCY: DIMENSIONS OF
DEVIANCE
                    edited by Marc Riedel and
                    Terence P. Thornberry

CRIME PREVENTION AND SOCIAL CONTROL
                    edited by Ronald L. Akers and
                    Edward Sagarin

IMAGES OF CRIME: Offenders and Victims
                    edited by Terence Thornberry and
                    Edward Sagarin

ISSUES IN CRIMINAL JUSTICE: PLANNING
AND EVALUATION
                    edited by Marc Riedel and
                    Pedro A. Vales

POLICE: PROBLEMS AND PROSPECTS
                    edited by Donal E. J. MacNamara and
                    Marc Riedel

POLITICS AND CRIME
                    edited by Sawyer Sylvester and
                    Edward Sagarin

TREATING THE OFFENDER: PROBLEMS
AND ISSUES
                    edited by Marc Riedel and
                    Pedro A. Vales